Twelfth Night

JOSEPH SOBRAN

mc **Marshall Cavendish**
Benchmark
New York

Series consultant: Richard Larkin

Marshall Cavendish
99 White Plains Road
Tarrytown, New York 10591
www.marshallcavendish.us

Library of Congress Cataloging-in-Publication Data
Sobran, Joseph.
Twelfth night / by Joseph Sobran.
p. cm. — (Shakespeare explained)
Includes bibliographical references and index.
Summary: "A literary analysis of Shakespeare's play Twelfth Night.
Includes information on the history and culture of Elizabethan
England"—Provided by publisher.
ISBN 978-0-7614-3425-2
1. Shakespeare, William, 1564-1616. Twelfth night—Juvenile literature.
2. England—Civilization—16th century—Juvenile literature.
I. Title. PR2837.S63 2009
822.3'3—dc22
2009007895

Photo research by: Linda Sykes
istockphoto: front cover; Bart Parren/istockphoto: 1; Neven Mendrila/Shutterstock: 3; Raciro/
istockphoto: 4; Art Parts RF: 6, 8, 13, 24, 25; Nik Wheeler/Corbis: 11; Portraitgalerie, Schloss
Ambras, Innsbruck, Austria/Erich Lessing/Art Resource, NY: 18; AA World Travel Library/Alamy:
20; Hideo Kurihara/Alamy: 22; Corbis/Sygma: 27; Andrew Fox/Corbis: 30; Royal Shakespeare
Company: 37; Private Collection/Barbara Singer/The Bridgeman Art Library: 41; Reg Wilson/Royal
Shakespeare Company: 44; Robbie Jack/Corbis: 47; David Ball, Angus McBean Studio/Royal
Shakespeare Theatre: 53; T. Charles Erickson: 56; Paul Doyle/Alamy: 58; Bildarchiv Preussischer
Kulturbesitz/Art Resource, NY: 62; Tristram Kenton/Lebrecht Music and Arts: 64;
Fine Line/Renaissance/The Kobal Collection: 73; allposters.com: 77.

Editor: Deborah Grahame
Publisher: Michelle Bisson
Art Director: Anahid Hamparian
Series Design: Kay Petronio

Printed in Malaysia
135642

Contents

Shakespeare and His World

WILLIAM SHAKESPEARE, OFTEN NICKNAMED "THE BARD," IS, BEYOND ANY COMPARISON, THE MOST TOWERING NAME IN ENGLISH LITERATURE. MANY CONSIDER HIS PLAYS THE GREATEST EVER WRITTEN. HE STANDS OUT EVEN AMONG GENIUSES.

Yet the Bard is also closer to our hearts than lesser writers, and his tremendous reputation should neither intimidate us nor prevent us from enjoying the simple delights he offers in such abundance. It is as if he had written for each of us personally. As he himself put it, "One touch of nature makes the whole world kin."

Such tragedies as *Hamlet*, *Romeo and Juliet*, and *Macbeth* are world famous, still performed onstage and in films. These and others have also been adapted for radio, television, opera, ballet, pantomime, novels, comic books, and other media. Two of the best ways to become familiar with them are to watch some of the many fine movies that have been made of them and to listen to recordings of them by some of the world's great actors.

Even Shakespeare's individual characters have lives of their own, like real historical figures. Hamlet is still regarded as the most challenging role ever written for an actor. Roughly as many whole books have been written about Hamlet, an imaginary character, as about actual historical figures such as Abraham Lincoln and Napoleon Bonaparte.

Shakespeare created an amazing variety of vivid characters. One of Shakespeare's most peculiar traits was that he loved his characters so much—even some of his villains and secondary or comic characters—that at times he let them run away with the play, stealing attention from his heroes and heroines.

So in *A Midsummer Night's Dream* audiences remember the absurd and lovable fool Bottom the Weaver better than the lovers who are the main characters. Romeo's friend Mercutio is more fiery and witty than Romeo himself; legend claims that Shakespeare said he had to kill Mercutio or Mercutio would have killed the play.

Shakespeare also wrote dozens of comedies and historical plays, as well as nondramatic poems. Although his tragedies are now regarded as his greatest works, he freely mixed them with comedy and history. And his sonnets are among the supreme love poems in the English language.

It is Shakespeare's mastery of the English language that keeps his words familiar to us today. Every literate person knows dramatic lines such as "Wherefore art thou Romeo?"; "My kingdom for a horse!"; "To be or not to be: that is the question"; "Friends, Romans, countrymen, lend me your ears"; and "What fools these mortals be!" Shakespeare's sonnets are noted for their sweetness: "Shall I compare thee to a summer's day?"

OUT OF THE JAWS OF DEATH.

SHAKESPEARE'S LANGUAGE

WITHOUT A DOUBT, SHAKESPEARE WAS THE GREATEST MASTER OF THE ENGLISH LANGUAGE WHO EVER LIVED. BUT JUST WHAT DOES THAT MEAN?

Shakespeare's vocabulary was huge, full of references to the Bible as well as Greek and Roman mythology. Yet his most brilliant phrases often combine very simple and familiar words:

"WHAT'S IN A NAME? THAT WHICH WE CALL A ROSE BY ANY OTHER NAME WOULD SMELL AS SWEET."

He has delighted countless millions of readers. And we know him only through his language. He has shaped modern English far more than any other writer.

Or, to put it in more personal terms, you probably quote his words several times every day without realizing it, even if you have never suspected that Shakespeare could be a source of pleasure to you.

So why do so many English-speaking readers find his language so difficult? It is our language, too, but it has changed so much that it is no longer quite the same language—nor a completely different one, either.

Shakespeare's English and ours overlap without being identical. He would have some difficulty understanding us, too! Many of our everyday words and phrases would baffle him.

Shakespeare, for example, would not know what we meant by a *car,* a *radio,* a *movie,* a *television,* a *computer,* or a *sitcom,* since these things did not even exist in his time. Our old-fashioned term *railroad train* would be unimaginable to him, far in the distant future. We would have to explain to him (if we could) what *nuclear weapons, electricity,* and *democracy* are. He would also be a little puzzled by common expressions such as *high-tech, feel the heat, approval ratings, war criminal, judgmental,* and *whoopie cushion.*

So how can we call him "the greatest master of the English language"? It might seem as if he barely spoke English at all! (He would, however, recognize much of our dirty slang, even if he pronounced it slightly differently. His plays also contain many racial insults to Jews, Africans, Italians, Irish, and others. Today he would be called "insensitive.")

Many of the words of Shakespeare's time have become archaic. Words like *thou, thee, thy, thyself,* and *thine,* which were among the most common words in the language in Shakespeare's day, have all but disappeared today. We simply say *you* for both singular and plural, formal and familiar. Most other modern languages have kept their *thou.*

Sometimes the same words now have different meanings. We are apt to be misled by such simple, familiar words as *kind, wonderful, waste, just,* and *dear,* which he often uses in ways that differ from our usage.

Shakespeare also doesn't always use the words we expect to hear, the words that we ourselves would naturally use. When we might automatically say, "I beg your pardon" or just "Sorry," he might say, "I cry you mercy."

Often a glossary and footnotes will solve all three of these problems for us. But it is most important to bear in mind that Shakespeare was often hard for his first audiences to understand. Even in his own time his rich language was challenging. And this was deliberate. Shakespeare was inventing his own kind of English. It remains unique today.

A child doesn't learn to talk by using a dictionary. Children learn first by sheer immersion. We teach babies by pointing at things and saying their names. Yet the toddler always learns faster than we can teach! Even as babies we are geniuses. Dictionaries can help us later, when we already speak and read the language well (and learn more slowly).

So the best way to learn Shakespeare is not to depend on the footnotes and glossary too much, but instead to be like a baby: just get into the flow of the language. Go to performances of the plays or watch movies of them.

THE LANGUAGE HAS A MAGICAL WAY OF TEACHING ITSELF, IF WE LET IT. THERE IS NO REASON TO FEEL STUPID OR FRUSTRATED WHEN IT DOESN'T COME EASILY.

Hundreds of phrases have entered the English language from *Hamlet* alone, including "to hold, as t'were, the mirror up to nature"; "murder most foul"; "the thousand natural shocks that flesh is heir to"; "flaming youth"; "a countenance more in sorrow than in anger"; "the play's the thing"; "neither a borrower nor a lender be"; "in my mind's eye"; "something is rotten in the state of Denmark"; "alas, poor Yorick"; and "the lady doth protest too much, methinks."

From other plays we get the phrases "star-crossed lovers"; "what's in a name?"; "we have scotched the snake, not killed it"; "one fell swoop"; "it was Greek to me"; "I come to bury Caesar, not to praise him"; and "the most unkindest cut of all"—all these are among our household words. In fact, Shakespeare even gave us the expression "household words." No wonder his contemporaries marveled at his "fine filed phrase" and swooned at the "mellifluous and honey-tongued Shakespeare."

Shakespeare's words seem to combine music, magic, wisdom, and humor:

"THE COURSE OF TRUE LOVE NEVER DID RUN SMOOTH."

"HE JESTS AT SCARS THAT NEVER FELT A WOUND."

"THE FAULT, DEAR BRUTUS, IS NOT IN OUR STARS, BUT IN OURSELVES, THAT WE ARE UNDERLINGS."

"COWARDS DIE MANY TIMES BEFORE THEIR DEATHS; THE VALIANT NEVER TASTE OF DEATH BUT ONCE."

"NOT THAT I LOVED CAESAR LESS, BUT THAT I LOVED ROME MORE."

"THERE ARE MORE THINGS IN HEAVEN AND EARTH, HORATIO, THAN ARE DREAMT OF IN YOUR PHILOSOPHY."

"BREVITY IS THE SOUL OF WIT."

"THERE'S A DIVINITY THAT SHAPES OUR ENDS, ROUGH-HEW THEM HOW WE WILL."

Four centuries after Shakespeare lived, to speak English is to quote him. His huge vocabulary and linguistic fertility are still astonishing. He has had a powerful effect on all of us, whether we realize it or not. We may wonder how it is even possible for a single human being to say so many memorable things.

Only the King James translation of the Bible, perhaps, has had a more profound and pervasive influence on the English language than Shakespeare. And, of course, the Bible was written by many authors over many centuries, and the King James translation, published in 1611, was the combined effort of many scholars.

EARLY LIFE

So who, exactly, was Shakespeare? Mystery surrounds his life, largely because few records were kept during his time. Some people have even doubted his identity, arguing that the real author of Shakespeare's plays must have been a man of superior formal education and wide experience. In a sense such doubts are a natural and understandable reaction to his rare, almost miraculous powers of expression, but some people feel that the doubts themselves show a lack of respect for the supremely human poet.

Most scholars agree that Shakespeare was born in the town of Stratford-upon-Avon in the county of Warwickshire, England, in April 1564. He was baptized, according to local church records, Gulielmus (William) Shakspere (the name was spelled in several different ways) on April 26 of that year. He was one of several children, most of whom died young.

His father, John Shakespeare (or Shakspere), was a glove maker and, at times, a town official. He was often in debt or being fined for unknown delinquencies, perhaps failure to attend church regularly. It is suspected that John was a recusant (secret and illegal) Catholic, but there is no proof. Many

SHAKESPEARE'S CHILDHOOD HOME IS CARED FOR BY AN INDEPENDENT CHARITY, THE SHAKESPEARE BIRTHPLACE TRUST, IN STRATFORD-UPON-AVON, WARWICKSHIRE, ENGLAND.

scholars have found Catholic tendencies in Shakespeare's plays, but whether Shakespeare was Catholic or not we can only guess.

At the time of Shakespeare's birth, England was torn by religious controversy and persecution. The country had left the Roman Catholic Church during the reign of King Henry VIII, who had died in 1547. Two of Henry's children, Edward and Mary, ruled after his death. When his daughter Elizabeth I became queen in 1558, she upheld his claim that the monarch of England was also head of the English Church.

Did William attend the local grammar school? He was probably entitled to, given his father's prominence in Stratford, but again, we face a frustrating absence of proof, and many people of the time learned to read very well without schooling. If he went to the town school, he would also have learned the rudiments of Latin.

We know very little about the first half of William's life. In 1582, when he was eighteen, he married Anne Hathaway, eight years his senior. Their first daughter, Susanna, was born six months later. The following year they had twins, Hamnet and Judith.

At this point William disappears from the records again. By the early 1590s we find "William Shakespeare" in London, a member of the city's leading acting company, called the Lord Chamberlain's Men. Many of Shakespeare's greatest roles, we are told, were first performed by the company's star, Richard Burbage.

Curiously, the first work published under (and identified with) Shakespeare's name was not a play but a long erotic poem, *Venus and Adonis*, in 1593. It was dedicated to the young Earl of Southampton, Henry Wriothesley.

Venus and Adonis was a spectacular success, and Shakespeare was immediately hailed as a major poet. In 1594 he dedicated a longer, more serious poem to Southampton, *The Rape of Lucrece*. It was another hit, and for many years, these two poems were considered Shakespeare's greatest works, despite the popularity of his plays.

LET THERE BE GALL ENOUGH IN THY INK.

SHAKESPEARE ON FILM: A SAMPLER

TODAY MOVIES, NOT LIVE PLAYS, ARE THE MORE POPULAR ART FORM. FORTUNATELY MOST OF SHAKESPEARE'S PLAYS HAVE BEEN FILMED, AND THE BEST OF THESE MOVIES OFFER AN EXCELLENT WAY TO MAKE THE BARD'S ACQUAINTANCE. RECENTLY, KENNETH BRANAGH HAS BECOME A RESPECTED CONVERTER OF SHAKESPEARE'S PLAYS INTO FILM.

Hamlet

Hamlet, Shakespeare's most famous play, has been well filmed several times. In 1948 Laurence Olivier won three Academy Awards—for best picture, best actor, and best director—for his version of the play. The film allowed him to show some of the magnetism that made him famous on the stage. Nobody spoke Shakespeare's lines more thrillingly.

The young Derek Jacobi played Hamlet in a 1980 BBC production of the play, with Patrick Stewart (now best known for *Star Trek, the Next Generation*) as the guilty king. Jacobi, like Olivier, has a gift for speaking the lines freshly; he never seems to be merely reciting the famous and familiar words. But whereas Olivier has animal passion, Jacobi is more intellectual. It is fascinating to compare the ways these two outstanding actors play Shakespeare's most complex character.

Franco Zeffirelli's 1990 *Hamlet*, starring Mel Gibson, is fascinating in a different way. Gibson, of course, is best known as an action hero, and he is not well suited to this supremely witty and introspective role, but Zeffirelli cuts the text drastically, and the result turns *Hamlet* into something that few people would have expected: a short, swiftly moving action movie. Several of the other characters are brilliantly played.

Henry IV, Part One

The 1979 BBC Shakespeare series production does a commendable job in this straightforward approach to the play. Battle scenes are effective despite obvious restrictions in an indoor studio setting. Anthony Quayle gives jovial Falstaff a darker edge, and Tim Pigott-Smith's Hotspur is buoyed by some humor. Jon Finch plays King Henry IV with noble authority, and David Gwillim gives Hal a surprisingly successful transformation from boy prince to heir apparent.

Julius Caesar

No really good movie of *Julius Caesar* exists, but the 1953 film, with Marlon Brando as Mark Antony, will do. James Mason is a thoughtful Brutus, and John Gielgud, then ranked with Laurence Olivier among the greatest Shakespearean actors, plays the villainous Cassius. The film is rather dull, and Brando is out of place in a Roman toga, but it is still worth viewing.

Macbeth

Roman Polanski is best known as a director of thrillers and horror films, so it may seem natural that he should have done his 1971 *The Tragedy of Macbeth* as an often-gruesome slasher flick. But this is also one of the most vigorous of all Shakespeare films. Macbeth and his wife are played by Jon Finch and Francesca Annis, neither known for playing Shakespeare, but they are young and attractive in roles that are usually given to older actors, which gives the story a fresh flavor.

The Merchant of Venice

Once again the matchless Sir Laurence Olivier delivers a great performance as Shylock with his wife Joan Plowright as Portia in the 1974 TV film, adapted from the 1970 National Theater (of Britain) production. A 1980 BBC offering features Warren Mitchell as Shylock and Gemma Jones as Portia, with John Rhys-Davies as Salerio. The most recent production, starring Al Pacino as Shylock, Jeremy Irons as Antonio, and Joseph Fiennes as Bassanio, was filmed in Venice and released in 2004.

A Midsummer Night's Dream

Because of the prestige of his tragedies, we tend to forget how many comedies Shakespeare wrote—nearly twice the number of tragedies. Of these perhaps the most popular has always been the enchanting, atmospheric, and very silly masterpiece *A Midsummer Night's Dream*.

In more recent times several films have been made of *A Midsummer Night's Dream*. Among the more notable have been Max Reinhardt's 1935 black-and-white version, with Mickey Rooney (then a child star) as Puck.

Of the several film versions, the one starring Kevin Kline as Bottom and Stanley Tucci as Puck, made in 1999 with nineteenth-century costumes and directed by Michael Hoffman, ranks among the finest, and is surely one of the most sumptuous to watch.

Othello

Orson Welles did a budget European version in 1952, now available as a restored DVD. Laurence Olivier's 1965 film performance is predictably remarkable, though it has been said that he would only approach the part by honoring, even emulating, Paul Robeson's definitive interpretation that ran on Broadway in 1943. (Robeson was the first black actor to play Othello, the Moor of Venice, and he did so to critical acclaim, though sadly his performance was never filmed.) Maggie Smith plays a formidable Desdemona opposite Olivier, and her youth and energy will surprise younger audiences who know her only from the Harry Potter films. Laurence Fishburne brilliantly portrayed Othello in the 1995 film, costarring with Kenneth Branagh as a surprisingly human Iago, though Irène Jacob's Desdemona was disappointingly weak.

Romeo and Juliet

This, the world's most famous love story, has been filmed many times, twice very successfully over the last generation. Franco Zeffirelli directed a hit version in 1968 with Leonard Whiting and the rapturously pretty Olivia Hussey, set in Renaissance Italy. Baz Luhrmann made a much more contemporary version, with a loud rock score, starring Leonardo DiCaprio and Claire Danes, in 1996.

It seems safe to say that Shakespeare would have preferred Zeffirelli's movie, with its superior acting and rich, romantic, sun-drenched Italian scenery.

The Tempest

A 1960 Hallmark Hall of Fame production featured Maurice Evans as Prospero, Lee Remick as Miranda, Roddy McDowall as Ariel, and Richard Burton as Caliban. The special effects are primitive and the costumes are ludicrous, but it moves along at a fast pace. Another TV version aired in 1998 and was nominated for a Golden Globe. Peter Fonda played Gideon Prosper, and Katherine Heigl played his daughter Miranda Prosper. Sci-fi fans may already know that the classic 1956 film *Forbidden Planet* is modeled on themes and characters from the play.

Twelfth Night

Trevor Nunn adapted the play for the 1996 film he also directed in a rapturous Edwardian setting, with big names like Helena Bonham Carter, Richard E. Grant, Imogen Stubbs, and Ben Kingsley as Feste. A 2003 film set in modern Britain provides an interesting multicultural experience; it features an Anglo-Indian cast with Parminder Nagra (*Bend It Like Beckham*) playing Viola. For the truly intrepid, a twelve-minute silent film made in 1910 does a fine job of capturing the play through visual gags and over-the-top gesturing.

THESE FILMS HAVE BEEN SELECTED FOR SEVERAL QUALITIES: APPEAL AND ACCESSIBILITY TO MODERN AUDIENCES, EXCELLENCE IN ACTING, PACING, VISUAL BEAUTY, AND, OF COURSE, FIDELITY TO SHAKESPEARE. THEY ARE THE MOTION PICTURES WE JUDGE MOST LIKELY TO HELP STUDENTS UNDERSTAND THE SOURCE OF THE BARD'S LASTING POWER.

Today we sometimes speak of "live entertainment." In Shakespeare's day, of course, all entertainment was live, because recordings, films, television, and radio did not yet exist. Even printed books were a novelty.

In fact, most communication in those days was difficult. Transportation was not only difficult but slow, chiefly by horse and boat. Most people were illiterate peasants who lived on farms that they seldom left; cities grew up along waterways and were subject to frequent plagues that could wipe out much of the population within weeks.

Money—in coin form, not paper—was scarce and hardly existed outside the cities. By today's standards, even the rich were poor. Life was precarious. Most children died young, and famine or disease might kill anyone at any time. Everyone was familiar with death. Starvation was not rare or remote, as it is to most of us today. Medical care was poor and might kill as many people as it healed.

This was the grim background of Shakespeare's theater during the reign of Queen Elizabeth I, who ruled from 1558 until her death in 1603. During that period England was also torn by religious conflict, often violent, among Roman

ELIZABETH I, A GREAT PATRON OF POETRY AND THE THEATER, WROTE SONNETS AND TRANSLATED CLASSIC WORKS.

Catholics who were loyal to the pope, adherents of the Church of England who were loyal to the queen, and the Puritans who would take over the country in the revolution of 1642.

Under these conditions, most forms of entertainment were luxuries that were out of most people's reach. The only way to hear music was to be in the actual physical presence of singers or musicians with their instruments, which were primitive by our standards.

One brutal form of entertainment, popular in London, was bearbaiting. A bear was blinded and chained to a stake, where fierce dogs called mastiffs were turned loose to tear him apart. The theaters had to compete with the bear gardens, as they were called, for spectators.

The Puritans, or radical Protestants, objected to bearbaiting and tried to ban it. Despite their modern reputation, the Puritans were anything but conservative. Conservative people, attached to old customs, hated them. They seemed to upset everything. (Many of America's first settlers, such as the Pilgrims who came over on the *Mayflower*, were dissidents who were fleeing the Church of England.)

Plays were extremely popular, but they were primitive, too. They had to be performed outdoors in the afternoon because of the lack of indoor lighting. Often the "theater" was only an enclosed courtyard. Probably the versions of Shakespeare's plays that we know today were not used in full, but shortened to about two hours for actual performance.

But eventually more regular theaters were built, featuring a raised stage extending into the audience. Poorer spectators (illiterate "groundlings") stood on the ground around it, at times exposed to rain and snow. Wealthier people sat in raised tiers above. Aside from some costumes, there were few props or special effects and almost no scenery. Much had to be imagined: Whole battles might be represented by a few actors with swords. Thunder might be simulated by rattling a sheet of tin offstage.

The plays were far from realistic and, under the conditions of the time, could hardly try to be. Above the rear of the main stage was a small balcony. (It was this balcony from which Juliet spoke to Romeo.) Ghosts and witches might appear by entering through a trapdoor in the stage floor.

Unlike the modern theater, Shakespeare's Globe Theater—he describes it as "this wooden O"—had no curtain separating the stage from the audience. This allowed intimacy between the players and the spectators.

THE RECONSTRUCTED GLOBE THEATER WAS COMPLETED IN 1997 AND IS LOCATED IN LONDON, JUST 200 YARDS (183 METERS) FROM THE SITE OF THE ORIGINAL.

WE WILL DRAW THE CURTAIN AND SHOW YOU THE PICTURE.

The spectators probably reacted rowdily to the play, not listening in reverent silence. After all, they had come to have fun! And few of them were scholars. Again, a play had to amuse people who could not read.

The lines of plays were written and spoken in prose or, more often, in a form of verse called iambic pentameter (ten syllables with five stresses per line). There was no attempt at modern realism. Only males were allowed on the stage, so some of the greatest women's roles ever written had to be played by boys or men. (The same is true, by the way, of the ancient Greek theater.)

Actors had to be versatile, skilled not only in acting, but also in fencing, singing, dancing, and acrobatics. Within its limitations, the theater offered a considerable variety of spectacles.

Plays were big business, not yet regarded as high art, sponsored by important and powerful people (the queen loved them as much as the groundlings did). The London acting companies also toured and performed in the provinces. When plagues struck London, the government might order the theaters to be closed to prevent the spread of disease among crowds. (They remained empty for nearly two years from 1593 to 1594.)

As the theater became more popular, the Puritans grew as hostile to it as they were to bearbaiting. Plays, like books, were censored by the government, and the Puritans fought to increase restrictions, eventually banning any mention of God and other sacred topics on the stage.

In 1642 the Puritans shut down all the theaters in London, and in 1644 they had the Globe demolished. The theaters remained closed until Charles's son, King Charles II, was restored to the throne in 1660 and the hated Puritans were finally vanquished.

But, by then, the tradition of Shakespeare's theater had been fatally interrupted. His plays remained popular, but they were often rewritten by inferior dramatists, and it was many years before they were performed (again) as he had originally written them.

THE ROYAL SHAKESPEARE THEATER, IN STRATFORD-UPON-AVON, WAS CLOSED IN 2007. A NEWLY DESIGNED INTERIOR WITH A 1,000-SEAT AUDITORIUM WILL BE COMPLETED IN 2010.

Today, of course, the plays are performed both in theaters and in films, sometimes in costumes of the period (ancient Rome for *Julius Caesar*, medieval England for *Henry V*), sometimes in modern dress (*Richard III* has recently been reset in England in the 1930s).

PLAYS

In the England of Queen Elizabeth I, plays were enjoyed by all classes of people, but they were not yet respected as a serious form of art.

Shakespeare's plays began to appear in print in individual, or quarto, editions in 1594, but none of these bore his name until 1598. Although his tragedies are now ranked as his supreme achievements, his name was first associated with comedies and with plays about English history.

The dates of Shakespeare's plays are notoriously hard to determine. Few performances of them were documented; some were not printed until decades after they first appeared on the stage. Mainstream scholars generally place most of the comedies and histories in the 1590s, admitting that this time frame is no more than a widely accepted estimate.

The three parts of *King Henry VI*, culminating in a fourth part, *Richard III*, deal with the long and complex dynastic struggle or civil wars known as the Wars of the Roses (1455–1487), one of England's most turbulent periods. Today it is not easy to follow the plots of these plays.

It may seem strange to us that a young playwright should have written such demanding works early in his career, but they were evidently very popular with the Elizabethan public. Of the four, only *Richard III*, with its wonderfully villainous starring role, is still often performed.

Even today, one of Shakespeare's early comedies, *The Taming of the Shrew*, remains a crowd-pleaser. (It has enjoyed success in a 1999 film adaptation, *10 Things I Hate About You*, with Heath Ledger and Julia Stiles.) The story is simple: The enterprising Petruchio resolves to marry a rich

THE "REAL" SHAKESPEARE

AROUND 1850 DOUBTS STARTED TO SURFACE ABOUT WHO HAD ACTUALLY WRITTEN SHAKESPEARE'S PLAYS, CHIEFLY BECAUSE MANY OTHER AUTHORS, SUCH AS MARK TWAIN, THOUGHT THE PLAYS' AUTHOR WAS TOO WELL EDUCATED AND KNOWLEDGEABLE TO HAVE BEEN THE MODESTLY SCHOOLED MAN FROM STRATFORD.

Who, then, was the real author? Many answers have been given, but the three leading candidates are Francis Bacon, Christopher Marlowe, and Edward de Vere, Earl of Oxford.

Francis Bacon (1561-1626)

Bacon was a distinguished lawyer, scientist, philosopher, and essayist. Many considered him one of the great geniuses of his time, capable of any literary achievement, though he wrote little poetry and, as far as we know, no dramas. When people began to suspect that "Shakespeare" was only a pen name, he seemed like a natural candidate. But his writing style was vastly different from the style of the plays.

Christopher Marlowe (1564–1593)

Marlowe wrote several excellent tragedies in a style much like that of the Shakespeare tragedies, though without the comic blend. But he was reportedly killed in a mysterious incident in 1593, before most of the Bard's plays existed. Could his death have been faked? Is it possible that he lived on for decades in hiding, writing under a pen name? This is what his advocates contend.

Edward de Vere, Earl of Oxford (1550–1604)

Oxford is now the most popular and plausible alternative to the lad from Stratford. He had a high reputation as a poet and playwright in his day, but his life was full of scandal. That controversial life seems to match what the poet says about himself in the sonnets, as well as many events in the plays (especially *Hamlet*). However, he died in 1604, and most scholars believe this rules him out as the author of plays that were published after that date.

THE GREAT MAJORITY OF EXPERTS REJECT THESE AND ALL OTHER ALTERNATIVE CANDIDATES, STICKING WITH THE TRADITIONAL VIEW, AFFIRMED IN THE 1623 FIRST FOLIO OF THE PLAYS, THAT THE AUTHOR WAS THE MAN FROM STRATFORD. THAT REMAINS THE SAFEST POSITION TO TAKE, UNLESS STARTLING NEW EVIDENCE TURNS UP, WHICH, AT THIS LATE DATE, SEEMS HIGHLY UNLIKELY.

young woman, Katherina Minola, for her wealth, despite her reputation for having a bad temper. Nothing she does can discourage this dauntless suitor, and the play ends with Kate becoming a submissive wife. It is all the funnier for being unbelievable.

With *Romeo and Juliet* the Bard created his first enduring triumph. This tragedy of "star-crossed lovers" from feuding families is known around the world. Even people with only the vaguest knowledge of Shakespeare are often aware of this universally beloved story. It has inspired countless similar stories and adaptations, such as the hit musical *West Side Story*.

By the mid-1590s Shakespeare was successful and prosperous, a partner in the Lord Chamberlain's Men. He was rich enough to buy New Place, one of the largest houses in his hometown of Stratford.

Yet, at the peak of his good fortune came the worst sorrow of his life: Hamnet, his only son, died in August 1596 at the age of eleven, leaving nobody to carry on his family name, which was to die out with his two daughters.

Our only evidence of his son's death is a single line in the parish burial register. As far as we know, this crushing loss left no mark on Shakespeare's work. As far as his creative life shows, it was as if nothing had happened. His silence about his grief may be the greatest puzzle of his mysterious life, although, as we shall see, others remain.

During this period, according to traditional dating (even if it must be somewhat hypothetical), came the torrent of Shakespeare's mightiest works. Among these was another quartet of English history plays, this one centering on the legendary King Henry IV, including *Richard II* and the two parts of *Henry IV*.

Then came a series of wonderful romantic comedies: *Much Ado About Nothing*, *As You Like It*, and *Twelfth Night*.

In 1598 the clergyman Francis Meres, as part of a larger work, hailed

ACTOR JOSEPH FIENNES PORTRAYED THE BARD IN THE 1998 FILM *SHAKESPEARE IN LOVE*, DIRECTED BY JOHN MADDEN.

Shakespeare as the English Ovid, supreme in love poetry as well as drama. "The Muses would speak with Shakespeare's fine filed phrase," Meres wrote, "if they would speak English." He added praise of Shakespeare's "sugared sonnets among his private friends." It is tantalizing; Meres seems to know something of the poet's personal life, but he gives us no hard information. No wonder biographers are frustrated.

Next the Bard returned gloriously to tragedy with *Julius Caesar*. In the play Caesar has returned to Rome in great popularity after his military triumphs. Brutus and several other leading senators, suspecting that Caesar means to make himself king, plot to assassinate him. Midway through the play, after the assassination, comes one of Shakespeare's most famous scenes. Brutus speaks at Caesar's funeral. But then Caesar's friend Mark Antony delivers a powerful attack on the conspirators, inciting the mob to fury. Brutus and the others, forced to flee Rome, die in the ensuing civil war. In the end the spirit of Caesar wins after all. If Shakespeare had written nothing after *Julius Caesar*, he would still have been remembered as one of the greatest playwrights of all time. But his supreme works were still to come.

Only Shakespeare could have surpassed *Julius Caesar*, and he did so with *Hamlet* (usually dated about 1600). King Hamlet of Denmark has died, apparently bitten by a poisonous snake. Claudius, his brother, has married the dead king's widow, Gertrude, and become the new king, to the disgust and horror of Prince Hamlet. The ghost of old Hamlet appears to young Hamlet, reveals that he was actually poisoned by Claudius, and demands revenge. Hamlet accepts this as his duty, but cannot bring himself to kill his hated uncle. What follows is Shakespeare's most brilliant and controversial plot.

The story of *Hamlet* is set against the religious controversies of the Bard's time. Is the ghost in hell or purgatory? Is Hamlet Catholic or Protestant? Can revenge ever be justified? We are never really given the answers to such questions. But the play reverberates with them.

THE KING'S MEN

In 1603 Queen Elizabeth I died, and King James VI of Scotland became King James I of England. He also became the patron of Shakespeare's acting company, so the Lord Chamberlain's Men became the King's Men. From this point on, we know less of Shakespeare's life in London than in Stratford, where he kept acquiring property.

In the later years of the sixteenth century Shakespeare had been a rather elusive figure in London, delinquent in paying taxes. From 1602 to 1604 he lived, according to his own later testimony, with a French immigrant family named Mountjoy. After 1604 there is no record of any London residence for Shakespeare, nor do we have any reliable recollection of him or his whereabouts by others. As always, the documents leave much to be desired.

Nearly as great as *Hamlet* is *Othello*, and many regard *King Lear*, the heartbreaking tragedy about an old king and his three daughters, as Shakespeare's supreme tragedy. Shakespeare's shortest tragedy, *Macbeth*, tells the story of a Scottish lord and his wife who plot to murder the king of Scotland to gain the throne for themselves. *Antony and Cleopatra*, a sequel to *Julius Caesar*, depicts the aging Mark Antony in love with the enchanting queen of Egypt. *Coriolanus*, another Roman tragedy, is the poet's least popular masterpiece.

SONNETS AND THE END

The year 1609 saw the publication of Shakespeare's Sonnets. Of these 154 puzzling love poems, the first 126 are addressed to a handsome young man, unnamed, but widely believed to be the Earl of Southampton; the rest concern a dark woman, also unidentified. These mysteries are still debated by scholars.

Near the end of his career Shakespeare turned to comedy again, but it was a comedy of a new and more serious kind. Magic plays a large role in these late plays. For example, in *The Tempest*, the exiled duke of Milan, Prospero, uses magic to defeat his enemies and bring about a final reconciliation.

According to the most commonly accepted view, Shakespeare, not yet fifty, retired to Stratford around 1610. He died prosperous in 1616 and left a will that divided his goods, with a famous provision leaving his wife "my second-best bed." He was buried in the chancel of the parish church, under a tombstone bearing a crude rhyme:

> GOOD FRIEND, FOR JESUS SAKE FORBEARE,
> TO DIG THE DUST ENCLOSED HERE.
> BLEST BE THE MAN THAT SPARES THESE STONES,
> AND CURSED BE HE THAT MOVES MY BONES.

This epitaph is another hotly debated mystery: did the great poet actually compose these lines himself?

SHAKESPEARE'S GRAVE IN HOLY TRINITY CHURCH, STRATFORD-UPON-AVON. HIS WIFE, ANNE HATHAWAY, IS BURIED BESIDE HIM.

THE FOLIO

In 1623 Shakespeare's colleagues of the King's Men produced a large volume of the plays (excluding the sonnets and other poems) titled *The Comedies, Histories, and Tragedies of Mr. William Shakespeare* with a woodcut portrait—the only known portrait—of the Bard. As a literary monument it is priceless, containing our only texts of half the plays; as a source of biographical information it is severely disappointing, giving not even the dates of Shakespeare's birth and death.

Ben Jonson, then England's poet laureate, supplied a long prefatory poem saluting Shakespeare as the equal of the great classical Greek tragedians Aeschylus, Sophocles, and Euripides, adding that "He was not of an age, but for all time."

Some would later denigrate Shakespeare. His reputation took more than a century to conquer Europe, where many regarded him as semi-barbarous. His works were not translated before 1740. Jonson himself, despite his personal affection, would deprecate "idolatry" of the Bard. For a time Jonson himself was considered more "correct" than Shakespeare, and possibly the superior artist.

But Jonson's generous verdict is now the whole world's. Shakespeare was not merely of his own age, "but for all time."

I AM SURE CARE'S AN ENEMY TO LIFE.

allegory—a story in which characters and events stand for general moral truths. Shakespeare never uses this form simply, but his plays are full of allegorical elements.

alliteration—repetition of one or more initial sounds, especially consonants, as in the saying "through thick and thin," or in Julius Caesar's statement, "veni, vidi, vici."

allusion—a reference, especially when the subject referred to is not actually named, but is unmistakably hinted at.

aside—a short speech in which a character speaks to the audience, unheard by other characters on the stage.

comedy—a story written to amuse, using devices such as witty dialogue (high comedy) or silly physical movement (low comedy). Most of Shakespeare's comedies were romantic comedies, incorporating lovers who endure separations, misunderstandings, and other obstacles but who are finally united in a happy resolution.

deus ex machina—an unexpected, artificial resolution to a play's convoluted plot. Literally, "god out of a machine."

dialogue—speech that takes place among two or more characters.

diction—choice of words for tone. A speech's diction may be dignified (as when a king formally addresses his court), comic (as when the ignorant grave diggers debate whether Ophelia deserves a religious funeral), vulgar, romantic, or whatever the dramatic occasion requires. Shakespeare was a master of diction.

Elizabethan—having to do with the reign of Queen Elizabeth I, from 1558 until her death in 1603. This is considered the most famous period in the history of England, chiefly because of Shakespeare and other noted authors (among them Sir Philip Sidney, Edmund Spenser, and Christopher Marlowe). It was also an era of military glory, especially the defeat of the huge Spanish Armada in 1588.

Globe—the Globe Theater housed Shakespeare's acting company, the Lord Chamberlain's Men (later known as the King's Men). Built in 1598, it caught fire and burned down during a performance of *Henry VIII* in 1613.

hyperbole—an excessively elaborate exaggeration used to create special emphasis or a comic effect, as in Montague's remark that his son Romeo's sighs are "adding to clouds more clouds" in *Romeo and Juliet*.

irony—a discrepancy between what a character says and what he or she truly believes, what is expected to happen and what really happens, or between what a character says and what others understand.

metaphor—a figure of speech in which one thing is identified with another, such as when Hamlet calls his father a "fair mountain." (See also **simile**.)

monologue—a speech delivered by a single character.

motif—a recurrent theme or image, such as disease in *Hamlet* or moonlight in *A Midsummer Night's Dream*.

oxymoron—a phrase that combines two contradictory terms, as in the phrase "sounds of silence" or Hamlet's remark, "I must be cruel only to be kind."

personification—imparting personality to something impersonal ("the sky wept"); giving human qualities to an idea or an inanimate object, as in the saying "love is blind."

pun—a playful treatment of words that sound alike, or are exactly the same, but have different meanings. In *Romeo and Juliet* Mercutio says, after being fatally wounded, "Ask for me tomorrow and you shall find me a grave man." *Grave* could mean either "a place of burial" or "serious."

simile—a figure of speech in which one thing is compared to another, usually using the word *like* or *as*. (See also **metaphor**.)

soliloquy—a speech delivered by a single character, addressed to the audience. The most famous are those of Hamlet, but Shakespeare uses this device frequently to tell us his characters' inner thoughts.

symbol—a visible thing that stands for an invisible quality, as poison in *Hamlet* stands for evil and treachery.

syntax—sentence structure or grammar. Shakespeare displays amazing variety of syntax, from the sweet simplicity of his songs to the clotted fury of his great tragic heroes, who can be very difficult to understand at a first hearing. These effects are deliberate; if we are confused, it is because Shakespeare means to confuse us.

theme—the abstract subject or message of a work of art, such as revenge in *Hamlet* or overweening ambition in *Macbeth*.

tone—the style or approach of a work of art. The tone of *A Midsummer Night's Dream*, set by the lovers, Bottom's crew, and the fairies, is light and sweet. The tone of *Macbeth*, set by the witches, is dark and sinister.

tragedy—a story that traces a character's fall from power, sanity, or privilege. Shakespeare's well-known tragedies include *Hamlet, Macbeth,* and *Othello*.

tragicomedy—a story that combines elements of both tragedy and comedy, moving a heavy plot through twists and turns to a happy ending.

verisimilitude—having the appearance of being real or true.

understatement—a statement expressing less than intended, often with an ironic or comic intention; the opposite of hyperbole.

SHAKESPEARE AND
TWELFTH NIGHT

Character sketches ▶
from an 1884 edition
of the *Illustrated News*
announcing the production
at the Lyceum Theater.

Chapter One

Shakespeare and Twelfth Night

THE DATES OF ALL SHAKESPEARE'S PLAYS ARE SOMEWHAT UNCERTAIN, BUT MOST SCHOLARS BELIEVE THAT *TWELFTH NIGHT* WAS WRITTEN AROUND 1600. IT WAS PERHAPS THE LAST OF HIS MOST CHEERFUL COMEDIES, FOLLOWING *MUCH ADO ABOUT NOTHING* AND *AS YOU LIKE IT* AND PRECEDING THE SERIES OF GREAT TRAGEDIES THAT BEGAN WITH *HAMLET*. AS ITS TITLE SEEMS TO SUGGEST, *TWELFTH NIGHT* MAY HAVE BEEN COMPOSED AND PERFORMED FOR THE CHRISTMAS SEASON AROUND THE TURN OF THE CENTURY, BUT THIS HAS NEVER BEEN SETTLED. THE PLAY'S POPULARITY HAS INCREASED OVER THE YEARS.

Twelfth Night shows off several of the Bard's peerless talents—for creating colorful characters, for ingenious plotting, for delicate romantic comedy, for hilarious scenes (especially the deception of Malvolio with the forged love letter), for farce (in the duel scene), for broad humor tinged with pathos, and for sheer eloquence. In Viola we meet one of Shakespeare's loveliest heroines. She belongs to his amazing gallery of young women, each with her own unmistakable personality, and like several of the others she adopts a masculine disguise to pursue her feminine strategy. Shakespeare endows these heroines with an unusual wit and, except for an occasional Ophelia, strength of will. And Viola is matched in good qualities by her twin brother, Sebastian, who is as manly as she is feminine. Both characters have a way of immediately inspiring love and loyalty. Shakespeare has a deep interest, evident in almost every one of his works, in the nature of the sexes. His hundreds of vivid characters include many of the greatest roles in the theater for both men and women.

Over the years, *Twelfth Night* has become one of Shakespeare's most beloved comedies, even though it contains no single memorably pictorial moment as some of his other plays do—such as Bottom with the ass's head in *A Midsummer Night's Dream*, Hamlet holding Yorick's skull, Romeo at Juliet's balcony, Falstaff in the tavern, or Mark Antony at Caesar's funeral. Its famous lines are relatively few, and none of its characters have the miraculous eloquence and vitality of a Hamlet or a Cleopatra. Yet at least one noted Shakespeare critic, Stephen Booth, ranks *Twelfth Night* as Shakespeare's supreme achievement.

Even in Shakespeare's day, critics remarked on the similarity between *Twelfth Night* and his earlier comedy *The Comedy of Errors*. But in the earlier play, there were *two* sets of twins (all male!) to maximize the comic confusion. *Twelfth Night* is a far more mature and poetic work, peopled with much more interesting characters.

THE PLAY'S THE THING

- OVERVIEW AND ANALYSIS

- LIST OF CHARACTERS

- ANALYSIS OF MAJOR CHARACTERS

A nineteenth-century ▶ advertisement for Robson and Crane's production at Haverly's Fifth Avenue Theater.

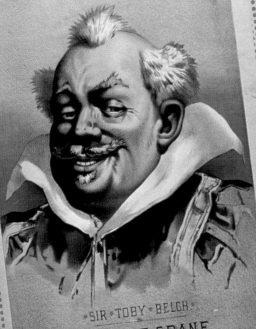

HAVERLY'S 5th AVE. THEA

Commencing Monday, Oct.

SIR · TOBY · BELCH ·

ROBSON & CRANE.
· IN · SHAKESPEARE'S ·
TWELFTH NIGHT

66929 **Chapter Two** 66929

CHAPTER TWO

The Play's the Thing

OVERVIEW

Orsino, Duke of Illyria, is lovesick for Countess Olivia, who is in mourning for her brother, who died shortly after their father died. Orsino is moodily listening to music with Curio, one of his servants, as the play begins ("If music be the food of love, play on," he commands his musicians), but he cuts the music short abruptly ("'Tis not so sweet now as it was before"). Valentine, another of Orsino's servants, whom he has sent to call on Olivia for him, returns to tell him that she is admitting no visitors now; she is planning to stay indoors until seven years have passed. This is how Olivia will keep her dear brother's memory alive. If she can be so devoted to a brother, Orsino reflects, Olivia will in time prove even more devoted to the right wooer—Orsino, of course.

ANALYSIS

This brief scene introduces the motifs of love and music. We learn that Orsino and Olivia are both sentimentalists, given to extravagant emotions about love. As always, Shakespeare uses economical means to provide essential information for the audience and to create a distinctive emotional atmosphere for his story.

ACT I, SCENE 2

OVERVIEW

Viola, along with a sea captain and sailors, arrives on the shore of Illyria after a shipwreck, in which her twin brother, Sebastian, has been lost. Viola fears he has drowned. The captain, however, saw Sebastian alive, bound to a mast of the split vessel; this gives Viola some hope that her brother has survived after all. The captain also tells Viola that Illyria is ruled by the duke Orsino. She knows the name and recalls that he used to be a bachelor. The captain adds that Orsino still is a bachelor, though he is rumored to be in love with the countess Olivia, who recently lost both her father and her brother. Viola asks the captain to help her disguise herself as a eunuch (a castrated male) so that she can find employment as a servant to Orsino. The captain agrees, and he decides to pose as Viola's mute. (This is the only time we hear of Viola's plan to pose as a eunuch; apparently she soon abandons the idea.)

ANALYSIS

Another brief scene sketches the situation for us. The brave Viola, one of Shakespeare's many twins surviving one of Shakespeare's many shipwrecks, forms her plan of action: disguising her sex (as many of Shakespeare's young women do), she will pose as a servant for Orsino.

A SHIPWRECKED VIOLA (ZOË WANAMAKER) TALKS WITH THE SEA CAPTAIN (JEREMY WILKIN) IN THE ROYAL SHAKESPEARE COMPANY'S 1983 PRODUCTION.

As usual, the Bard shows his great skill in exposition, quickly and clearly providing the basic facts we need in order to follow a story that will soon become complex, as Viola, one of his most charming and ingenious heroines, mediates between Orsino and Olivia. Yet Viola's very first remark about the duke—she recalls that he used to be a bachelor—is a tip-off to how the play will end.

Like Olivia, Viola has (apparently) lost a brother. Unlike Olivia, however, she does not let her grief paralyze her. From the first moment she hears the name Orsino, she notes that he was unmarried when she last heard of him, and she quickly resolves to seek employment with him by disguising her sex. Already we sense her possible romantic interest in this eligible duke.

ACT 1, SCENE 3

OVERVIEW

At Olivia's house, Sir Toby Belch, Olivia's loud, hard-drinking uncle, and Maria, her tiny servant, are discussing their mistress. Sir Toby complains that his niece is taking her brother's death very hard. Maria scolds him for keeping such late hours and provoking Olivia by drinking so much. Maria says Olivia has been objecting not only to Sir Toby's unruly life, but also to a certain "foolish knight," Sir Andrew Aguecheek, whom Sir Toby has brought into the household to woo Olivia during her mourning period. Sir Toby defends Sir Andrew, who is rich. (We quickly realize that Sir Toby is a shameless parasite, living off both Sir Toby and Olivia.)

Sir Andrew arrives, and his confused words to Maria expose him as a fool. But Sir Toby humors Sir Andrew with absurd compliments. When Sir Andrew speaks of leaving because he thinks he has no chance of winning Olivia—after all, Duke Orsino is trying to win her, too—Sir Toby encourages Sir Andrew to stay in the house. Sir Toby tells Sir Andrew that Olivia refuses to be wooed by the duke. Sir Andrew is too obtuse to see that, under the profuse praise, Sir Toby is mocking him. As the scene ends, the two knights look forward to reveling together.

Sir Andrew offers a bit of comic self-analysis: "I am a great eater of beef, and I believe that does harm to my wit." This comment shows he is dimly aware that he is a dimwit.

ANALYSIS

Here we enter the countess Olivia's house, where most of the play's central action takes place. Shakespeare gives us an intimate look at some of that household's wilder characters. We make the acquaintance of the playful Maria, the drunken Sir Toby, and the luckless Sir Andrew, three perpetrators of the play's great prank. (We have not yet met one of the chief characters, Malvolio, the target of their comic conspiracy.)

ACT I, SCENE 4

OVERVIEW

At the duke's palace, Viola, disguised as a page named Cesario, has become a servant to Orsino. She wins the duke's trust so quickly (in only three days, Valentine marvels) that he sends her to see Olivia on his behalf. When she protests that Olivia will refuse to see her, Orsino, thinking she is a "lad," assures her that her resemblance to a girl, in looks and voice, will make Olivia receptive. But Viola, we are not surprised to learn, has secretly fallen in love with Orsino herself!

ANALYSIS

The sweet and resourceful Viola shows herself equal to the challenges presented to her. She must handle delicate relations with both Orsino and Olivia, while concealing both her identity and her gender. In addition, she has her own passion to deal with: can she win Orsino's heart? If she can, she may move all the way from the lowly position of page to duchess of Illyria—though it is really Orsino's heart that she craves, not the title. Yet it is notable, and entirely to Viola's credit, that she is absolutely loyal to Orsino, and she never even thinks of undermining his courtship of another woman—although, in her position, it would be easy for her to do so.

ACT 1, SCENE 5

OVERVIEW

At Olivia's house, Maria tells Feste, Olivia's fool, that Olivia is angry with him because of his long and unexplained absence from her household. The pair are swapping jokes as Olivia arrives with her stern steward, Malvolio. Feste jests with Olivia too, playfully arguing that she, not he, is the real fool:

OLIVIA (JANIE DEE) AND FESTE (CLIVE ROWE) SHARE THE STAGE AT THE OPEN AIR THEATER IN LONDON'S REGENT PARK, 2008.

Why is Olivia in mourning if she is so certain that her brother's soul is in heaven?

Delighted, Olivia asks Malvolio how he likes this jester. He replies, with his own sour wit, that Feste is lacking in brains. Feste easily turns Malvolio's insults against him. Olivia defends her fool and attacks the priggish (offensive) steward: "O, you are sick of self-love, Malvolio, and taste with a distempered appetite." Feste welcomes her reproof to the steward with joyous humor.

Maria enters to tell Olivia that a messenger from Orsino is at the door, and the half-drunk Sir Toby is trying to hold him off. Olivia orders Malvolio to get rid of the messenger—if he comes from Orsino—with the excuse that she is sick. Malvolio returns to tell her that the "gentleman" (who is actually Viola) refuses to accept any excuses and insists on seeing her. At last, putting on a veil, Olivia agrees to let the messenger in.

Viola comes in and speaks with Olivia alone, telling her of Orsino's ardent love for her. Olivia says she cannot love Orsino ("Let him send no more"). Thanking Viola for her trouble, Olivia offers her money, but Viola will not accept cash. Viola departs.

Olivia, mistaking Viola for a boy, has fallen in love with her! (So much for Olivia's resolution to remain cloistered for seven years!) Hoping to entice Cesario to return, she summons Malvolio and gives him a ring that she says Viola has left with her. Olivia orders him to chase Viola and return it to "that same peevish messenger."

ANALYSIS

This scene develops one of the play's central themes: the confusion of the sexes that will provide so much of the fun (as well as seriousness). We meet the grumpy steward Malvolio, whom it is so tempting to dislike, in spite of the very real virtues Olivia esteems in him. He is not, after all, an evil man; on the contrary, he is honest and trustworthy, and he harms

MANY A GOOD HANGING PREVENTS A BAD MARRIAGE.

nobody. Even his enemies recognize that he is virtuous, even if, like most of Shakespeare's villains, he doesn't know how to have fun. Malvolio reminds us that virtue is not always amiable. Can he be blamed if Olivia delegates to him the tasks she prefers not to do herself? We resent him merely for doing his duty.

We are not told how long Malvolio has been a steward. He does not seem new to the position; was he employed by Olivia's father and brother too? We can only guess. Olivia certainly has high regard for him, though she is quick to scold him when she thinks it appropriate.

It may also be worth bearing in mind that Olivia lost both her father and her brother only recently, so she has not held her estate for very long. Yet she rules it with intelligence and authority, and she is determined not to let her dissolute uncle, Sir Toby, take advantage of her.

Illyria is still part of the feudal world, where most people keep the status they were born with and social mobility is very limited. This is why Malvolio's secret ambition to marry Olivia is so comical. Olivia herself puts her finger on his weakness: self-love.

With a little nudge, Malvolio will be revealed as the social climber he secretly is. Even before he reads the fateful forged letter, he is pondering the encouraging example of another servant who married above himself.

ACT II, SCENE 1

OVERVIEW

Viola's twin brother, Sebastian, is with Antonio, another sea captain, on the coast of Illyria. Sebastian has survived the shipwreck but thinks his sister has perished in the storm. He resolves to go to Orsino's court, but Antonio, who remembers that he has "many enemies" there, is at first afraid to go with him. Yet when Sebastian sets out for the palace, Antonio follows him, in spite of the danger to himself.

ANALYSIS

This brief scene confirms that Viola's twin brother has survived the shipwreck. Like Viola, Sebastian inspires affection, even devotion. Antonio is already willing to risk his own life to help his handsome and charming young friend, who believes his lovely sister has drowned. Antonio's love for Sebastian adds one more strand to what is becoming a complex plot.

In fact, some critics rank the plot of *Twelfth Night* as Shakespeare's most ingenious. Though it has no fairies, witches, oracles, or other supernatural elements, it does contain devices found in many of the Bard's other comedies: a shipwreck, separated twins, and a heroine in masculine disguise. These are ancient stage conventions, and it matters very little whether or not they are actually plausible.

Shakespeare's artistry and mastery of drama are evident in the way he shows us so early that Sebastian has survived the shipwreck. If Shakespeare had delayed this revelation until late in the play, it would seem to us an implausible coincidence. By telling us at the beginning of the second act and frequently reminding us of it, he prepares us for later story developments that we might otherwise find hard to accept.

ACT II, SCENE 2

OVERVIEW

Malvolio overtakes Viola in the street and demands that she take the ring. Naturally this confuses her for a moment, because she did not leave a ring with Olivia. With some annoyance, Malvolio throws it down and leaves Viola to pick it up if she wants to.

When Viola is alone, it dawns on her what this means: Olivia, mistaking Viola's sex, has fallen in love with her! A fine kettle of fish this is: Viola loves Orsino, who loves Olivia, who loves Viola! And the confusion is just beginning.

ANALYSIS

Poor Viola, in love with her master Orsino, now finds that the great lady he has sent her to woo has fallen in love with her in her male disguise! She is becoming more and more keenly aware of the curious position she occupies—she even calls herself a "monster" who belongs to both sexes at once. She sums up her own plight in a soliloquy:

> WHAT WILL BECOME OF THIS? AS I AM MAN,
> MY STATE IS DESPERATE FOR MY MASTER'S LOVE;
> AS I AM WOMAN (NOW ALAS THE DAY!),
> WHAT THRIFTLESS SIGHS SHALL POOR OLIVIA BREATHE!
> O TIME, THOU MUST UNTANGLE THIS, NOT I,
> IT IS TOO HARD A KNOT FOR ME T'UNTIE.

ACT II, SCENE 3

OVERVIEW

Sir Toby and Sir Andrew, both drunk, are reveling after midnight in Olivia's house when Feste joins them. The three join in merry fooling until Sir Andrew calls for a love song. After Feste sings one, the noise they are making brings Maria, who scolds them with the warning that Olivia will send Malvolio to throw them out. The drunken men reply with defiant humor as Maria pleads in vain for quiet.

Sure enough, Malvolio comes in. Furious at the unseemly din, he asks if they have no sense of time. When Sir Toby answers with a jest, the angry steward singles Toby out for a special rebuke as Olivia's kinsman, threatening to expel him unless he mends his rowdy ways. This fails to quell the knight's insolence. He and Feste sing snatches of a ballad mocking Malvolio, and Sir Toby asks the haughty steward, in a famous sarcasm, "Dost thou think, because thou art virtuous, there shall be no more cakes and ale?" Then Sir Toby orders Maria to bring him some wine. As she obeys, Malvolio says he will report her to Olivia, and he departs in a fury.

Led by Maria, the incensed revelers agree on a plot against Malvolio. Maria says she can fake Olivia's handwriting well enough to fool Olivia herself, so she proposes to forge a love letter to Malvolio, causing him to think Olivia is in love with him and inviting him to woo her. Delighted with the prank, they part. Sir Toby, remarking that it is too late to go to bed now, tells Sir Andrew to get more money. It is finally dawning on Sir Andrew that he may not win Olivia's hand, but the greedy Sir Toby keeps giving him false encouragement.

ANALYSIS

The full impact of this rowdy scene is hard to figure out from reading it on the page. Sir Toby, Sir Andrew, and Feste are carousing when Maria comes to caution them that they will arouse Malvolio, but she soon joins in the fun herself, just as Malvolio makes his appearance.

ACT II, SCENE 4

OVERVIEW

Again Orsino calls for music in his palace, this time from Cesario (Viola). Curio tells him that Feste, whom Olivia's father loved and the one who should sing the old song, is absent. Orsino sends for Feste as the music plays, and while Curio goes to fetch Feste, Orsino tells Cesario to "remember me" if he ever falls in love, for, he boasts, he is constant, like all true lovers. Orsino asks, "How dost thou like this tune?" When Cesario praises it, Orsino asks if Cesario has ever been in love. When Cesario says yes, Orsino asks how old the woman was. "About your years, my lord," Viola says carefully. Orsino disapproves; a husband, he says, should always be older than his wife.

Curio returns with Feste, whom Orsino asks to sing the old tune they heard the previous night, one of the Bard's most famous lyrics, "Come Away, Death." Orsino tries to pay him for the entertainment, but Feste refuses the money and leaves.

When Orsino is alone with Viola, he commands her to go again to Olivia and proclaim his love. But, Viola asks, what if Olivia cannot love him in return? Orsino cuts her short: he will never accept such an answer. But

VIOLA (VIVIEN LEIGH) AND ORSINO (KEITH MITCHELL) IN THE ROYAL SHAKESPEARE COMPANY'S 1955 PRODUCTION DIRECTED BY JOHN GIELGUD

"SOME ARE BORN GREAT, SOME ACHIEVE GREATNESS,"

Viola says Orsino may have no choice in the matter, just as, if some woman loved him, she might have to accept his inability to love her in return. But Orsino refuses to admit even the idea that any woman could love him as ardently as he loves Olivia; no woman, he insists, could ever love that much. Viola disputes this. She says that her own father had a daughter who loved a man but never revealed her love and instead pined away silently for him—and this proves that women love more deeply than men. Of course Viola is secretly talking about herself and Orsino, but he misses her hidden meaning. He hands her a jewel to take to Olivia with the message that his love can endure no refusal.

ANALYSIS

Viola's plight is dramatized in this scene. As Cesario, she is bound to serve and obey Orsino, even when he commands her to help him woo Olivia. She is careful to speak ambiguously, often telling Orsino the truth so ingeniously that he fails to recognize her real meaning. Her position is both awkward and painful, and her selfless behavior—doing her best to help Orsino win Olivia's hand—commands both our respect and our sympathy.

ACT II, SCENE 5

OVERVIEW

In Olivia's garden, Sir Toby, Sir Andrew, and Fabian (a member of the household) look forward gleefully to the prank on Malvolio. Maria comes to alert them that Malvolio is on his way. She leaves; the others all hide as he enters, talking to himself.

As it happens, Malvolio at that moment is daydreaming aloud of marrying Olivia. He recalls that Maria once claimed Olivia liked him, and at another time Olivia herself told him that if she were attracted to a man, it would be to someone who looked like Malvolio. This is enough to amuse the three pranksters greatly as they eavesdrop on his soliloquy; they can barely keep quiet. Sir Toby nearly explodes in anger and laughter when Malvolio imagines himself a man of high rank: "Count Malvolio"! (We must remember that a steward was, after all, a mere servant.) The reverie goes on, as Malvolio imagines himself Olivia's husband, loftily ordering his servants to summon "my kinsman Toby" and Toby obediently curtseying to him. Overhearing all this, Sir Toby is nearly beside himself with fury at the steward's presumption. It gets no better when Malvolio pictures himself ordering "Cousin Toby" to "amend your drunkenness" and cease wasting time with a "foolish knight." (Sir Andrew, shrewd as ever, recognizes himself in this description: "I knew 'twas I, for many do call me fool.")

Just then Malvolio sees the forged letter. He picks it up and thinks he recognizes Olivia's handwriting. He reads it eagerly and takes the bait exactly as the pranksters have hoped. He also thinks he recognizes the letter's phrasing as Olivia's. The whole thing seems to refer to him in a code he has no trouble interpreting. "Some are born great," the letter says, "some achieve greatness, and some have greatness thrust upon 'em." It goes on to urge Malvolio to dress absurdly in yellow stockings, cross-gartered, and not to resist his good fortune unless he wants to remain a mere steward, stuck with the other servants all his life.

"AND SOME HAVE GREATNESS THRUST UPON 'EM.

ACTORS INTERPRET ACT II, SCENE 5 AS A GAME SHOW AT HOUSTON'S ALLEY THEATER, 2004.

Malvolio is ecstatic, exulting that "my lady loves me"! The letter's meaning is undeniable. Then he notices the postscript. It urges him to smile if he welcomes her (presumably Olivia's) love. The sour-faced Malvolio, now enraptured with hopes, promises to smile constantly.

When Malvolio has gone, Sir Toby, Sir Andrew, and Fabian roar with delight at Maria's inspired trick, so perfectly put into practice. They congratulate her as she reappears at that moment. She invites them to watch the rest of the prank as Malvolio greets Olivia in his new garb— which she is sure to hate, for she dislikes yellow stockings, loathes cross-gartering, and, being in mourning for her brother, will be in no mood for her steward's excessive smiling.

ANALYSIS

The hoax not only succeeds brilliantly, but also exposes Malvolio's secret nature: besides hiding a huge ego under his very proper exterior, he has a romantic heart that longs not just for power and status, but simply for love. In a way, this exposure of normal human weakness under an icy exterior will be Malvolio's deepest humiliation of all, since he pretends to be better than everyone else. ("You are idle shallow things. I am not of your element.")

ACT III, SCENE 1

OVERVIEW

Still in Olivia's garden, Viola/Cesario banters with Feste, who says he is not Olivia's fool, since she has no folly, but is instead her "corrupter of words." Despite their duel of wits, their mutual respect is clear. As Feste departs, leaving Viola alone, she muses that this apparent fool is indeed a wise man. Even feigning folly, she reflects, requires "a kind of wit."

Sir Toby and Sir Andrew arrive, and Sir Toby invites Viola into Olivia's house just as Olivia and Maria enter. Viola says her message must be to Olivia alone, so Olivia—always taking Viola for Cesario—dismisses Maria, Sir Toby, and Sir Andrew. Olivia asks, "What is your name?" Viola answers, "Cesario is your servant's name, fair princess." No, says Olivia, you are Orsino's servant. Viola responds that, because Orsino is Olivia's servant, his servant must also be her servant. Olivia reminds Viola that she does not wish to speak of Orsino anymore, and also reminds her of the ring that she pretended, with a "shameful cunning," to have received at their earlier meeting. After more wordplay, Olivia fervently confesses that she is in love with Cesario:

> CESARIO, BY THE ROSES OF THE SPRING,
> BY MAIDHOOD, HONOR, TRUTH, AND EVERYTHING,
> I LOVE THEE SO THAT, MAUGRE ALL THY PRIDE,
> NOR WIT NOR REASON CAN MY PASSION HIDE.

Cesario replies that "he" has only a single heart, which no woman shall ever possess "save I alone" (a nicely ambiguous answer—literally true, yet keeping her sexual identity concealed). Olivia invites Cesario to come again to plead for Orsino's love, though she now "abhors" it.

OLIVIA (KATE FLEETWOOD, LEFT), GETS FLIRTATIOUS AS VIOLA (LAURA REES, RIGHT) STANDS BY, AT THE CHICHESTER FESTIVAL THEATER'S 2007 PRODUCTION.

ANALYSIS

This scene deepens the play's themes of the nature of the sexes and the contrast between wit and folly. In Shakespeare's day, the word *wit* had a broader set of meanings than it has now. It included not only humor and cleverness, but also intelligence, reasoning ability, sanity, insight, and wisdom. (The term *halfwit* is now used only as an insult, but it used to describe a person who was mentally disabled. It was not considered offensive.)

The clown Feste and the disguised Viola banter in the wordplay so typical of Shakespeare, especially in this play, which abounds in puns, silly logic, tautologies, mock scholarship, and other amusing verbal devices. Feste, who describes himself as a "corrupter of words," remarks that "words are grown so false, I am loath to prove reason with them."

Alone with Olivia a few moments later, Viola still makes a game of speaking in riddles, telling the lady that "you do think you are not what you are" and "I am not what I am." These hints of Viola's disguise, of course, go over Olivia's head. When Olivia's love for Cesario is unrequited, she finds herself in the same position as Orsino, whose love she has scorned.

ACT III, SCENE 2

OVERVIEW

At last realizing that he has no chance of winning Olivia's hand, Sir Andrew threatens to leave her household and return home. He says plaintively that she has shown more favor to Orsino's servant, Cesario, than to him. Sir Toby and Fabian try to persuade Sir Andrew to stay longer. Fabian argues that Olivia's favor to Cesario was meant only to make Sir Andrew jealous, but he missed his opportunity. Sir Toby picks up this theme, telling the foolish knight that he can win Olivia with a display of manliness. Sir Andrew must write a letter to Cesario, insulting him and challenging him to a duel.

Sir Andrew falls for this scheme and leaves the two men, who agree laughingly that both he and Cesario will be too cowardly to fight. All that remains is to provoke Cesario, too.

Maria enters, also laughing. She summons Sir Toby and Fabian to come and enjoy the comical spectacle of Malvolio, dressed outlandishly for Olivia and behaving according to the terms of the forged letter.

ANALYSIS

This scene advances the plot in two respects.

First, we learn that Sir Andrew is realizing—better late than never—that he is wasting his time trying to win Olivia's favor; she obviously prefers Cesario. In order to prevent Sir Andrew from leaving, Sir Toby urges him to impress Olivia with his valor by challenging Cesario to a duel, which Sir Toby assumes that both men will be afraid to fight. This prepares us for a surprise when the scheme goes wrong. Sir Andrew goes off to write a challenge.

Second, we learn that Malvolio has been completely taken in by Maria's forged letter. The hoax has been a triumph. Three men now aspire to marry Olivia—Orsino, Sir Andrew, and Malvolio. But they are all destined to fail, for she loves only Cesario—who, of course, can never marry her.

OVERVIEW

Viola's twin brother, Sebastian, comes to a street near Orsino's urban estate. He is accompanied by the sea captain Antonio, who has joined him against Sebastian's wishes at great risk to himself. The grateful Sebastian urges Antonio to take care for his own safety. Antonio gives Sebastian money, and the two agree to meet later at an inn called the Elephant.

WHY, THIS IS VERY MIDSUMMER MADNESS.

ANALYSIS

In this scene the Bard lays the groundwork for several dramatic turns: the reunion of the twins, the duel between Sir Andrew and Cesario, and, most unexpectedly, the sudden marriage of Olivia, in spite of her vow to remain single for seven years in mourning for her brother.

Sebastian's survival from the shipwreck might have been a loose end in the plot of the play, but Shakespeare ingeniously builds a whole subplot on it, so that it strikes us as almost inevitable rather than arbitrary.

ACT III, SCENE 4

OVERVIEW

As Olivia and Maria enter Olivia's garden together, Olivia says in an aside that she has sent after "him" (Cesario) but is unsure how she should deal with him. She asks Maria how Malvolio is. Maria tells her that he appears to be possessed, out of his wits, for he does nothing but smile madly. Olivia tells Maria to bring him to her.

When Maria returns with Malvolio, the steward is indeed behaving oddly. His dress follows the instructions in the letter, yellow stockings and all. He addresses Olivia amorously, clearly thinking his bizarre romantic hints are welcome as he smiles and kisses his own hand repeatedly. Olivia is baffled; this is not at all the old Malvolio she has come to know. Maria leads him on as he keeps quoting the words of the forged letter, which of course mean nothing to Olivia, who sizes up his outlandish conduct as "very midsummer madness."

MALVOLIO PRESENTS HIMSELF IN YELLOW STOCKINGS TO THE COUNTESS IN A NINETEENTH-CENTURY LITHOGRAPH BY DANIEL MACLISE.

A servant announces the arrival of Orsino's young gentleman (Cesario). Olivia says she will go to him, but first she orders Maria to take care of Malvolio and make sure her people, including Sir Toby, see that no harm comes to him.

Malvolio, naturally, misconstrues Olivia's concern and thinks she is simply following her own prescriptions in the letter. He is flattered that no less a man than Sir Toby is (as he imagines) being put at his disposal. When Sir Toby, Fabian, and Maria enter, appealing to him to resist the devil that possesses him, he takes it all the wrong way and insults them ("You are idle shallow things; I am not of your element"). He tells them to go hang themselves as he rushes out in a rage.

The three pranksters savor their victory over the steward, and Sir Toby proposes that Malvolio be treated as a madman—bound and confined in a dark room for the time being, since Olivia already believes that he has lost his wits.

Sir Andrew rushes in excitedly, eager to show the others the challenge he has written to Cesario. Sir Toby, vastly amused at the success of this new trick, pretends to approve of the foolish knight's boldness and encourages him to keep it up. When Sir Andrew is gone, he says he will not deliver the letter to young Cesario, but instead will report to him that the knight is in a terrible fury. When he is finished with them, both of the prospective combatants will be far too frightened of each other to have a duel.

Olivia and Cesario enter, and the others depart. Olivia gives Cesario a jewel with her picture in it and beseeches the "servant" to come again the next day. Viola/Cesario accepts this gift as tactfully as she can, for her master's sake. Olivia exits.

Sir Toby and Fabian enter. They warn Cesario that Sir Andrew is a dreadful and furious adversary. Cesario protests that "he" has done nothing, as far as "he" knows, to offend anyone. Sir Toby answers that this does not matter; the brawling knight has already killed three men, and only more deaths will satisfy his present wrath.

MORE MATTER FOR A MAY MORNING.

"I am no fighter," Cesario objects, hoping that Olivia can afford "him" some protection. But Sir Toby continues to make Sir Andrew sound formidable, as does Fabian when Sir Toby leaves: "He is indeed, sir, the most skillful, bloody, and fatal opposite that you could possibly have found in any part of Illyria." Still, Fabian promises to make peace with Sir Andrew if he can.

VIOLA (KANANU KIRIMI) FENCES WITH SIR ANDREW AGUECHEEK (JOHN MACKAY) IN THE ROYAL SHAKESPEARE THEATER'S 2005 PRODUCTION.

As Fabian exits with the frightened Cesario, Sir Toby comes back with the equally frightened Sir Andrew, who says that if his enemy will abandon the duel he may have Sir Andrew's horse, Capilet. Cesario and Fabian return; Cesario and Sir Andrew, both goaded by Sir Toby (who assures each that there is really nothing to be afraid of), draw their swords on each other.

Now Antonio arrives! Mistaking Viola for her twin brother Sebastian, he tells Sir Andrew to put up his sword, or he will fight for his young friend. Sir Toby also draws his sword, just as a group of officers comes to arrest Antonio on Orsino's behalf. Now Antonio is angry with Viola, who he thinks has been ungrateful for Antonio's kindnesses (the money he lent Sebastian, for instance).

When Antonio heatedly addresses Viola as Sebastian, her heart beats faster. Can this mean that her dear Sebastian has not drowned, but is still alive after all? It seems too good to be true!

As Cesario exits, Sir Andrew is encouraged by the "boy's" display of cowardice and renews his challenge to a duel.

ANALYSIS

This long scene is full of comic misunderstandings. Malvolio has been misled by the fake letter; his behavior baffles Olivia, who knows nothing of the letter he supposes she wrote. She thinks he has gone mad. Maria, the letter's real author, is amused by all of this and stays silent about the prank.

"If this were played upon a stage now, I could condemn it as an improbable fiction," says Fabian of the prank on Malvolio. This is Shakespeare's comment on his own play. It *is* being acted on the stage, and it *is* an improbable fiction. This remark serves to express, in a humorous way, the audience's feelings about the unrealistic nature of the theater. We may be reminded of Theseus's wise words in *A Midsummer Night's Dream*: "The best in this kind are but shadows"—that is, even the best plays are only make-believe.

OVERVIEW

Near Olivia's house, Sebastian is trying to get rid of Feste. Feste has followed him, mistaking him for Cesario, whom Olivia has asked him to bring to her. Feste rejects Sebastian's denials that his name is Cesario. Sebastian pays the fool to go away and threatens to give him some "worse payment" unless he obeys.

Sir Andrew now appears, with Sir Toby and Fabian. He mistakes Sebastian for the timid Cesario and gives him a blow, which Sebastian instantly gives him back, with the question, "Are all the people mad?" Sir Toby seizes Sebastian and tells him to hold. Feste says he will report all of them to Olivia, and she will punish them. As Sebastian frees himself from Sir Toby's grip, the two men draw their swords.

Olivia enters and furiously orders her uncle to desist; she rebukes him for his extremely bad manners and apologizes to Sebastian. Overwhelmed by Olivia's sweet welcome, Sebastian thinks he must be dreaming.

Olivia has mistaken Sebastian for Cesario. She asks him to go with her to her house. He is startled, but he gladly agrees to be ruled by her.

ANALYSIS

The play moves boisterously toward its conclusion, when all these misunderstandings will be duly corrected. As yet, nobody knows that

"LEAVE THY VAIN BIBBLE-BABBLE."

Cesario is a girl, let alone that she has a twin brother. One way or another, nearly everyone but Viola is deceived by appearances.

ACT IV, SCENE 2

OVERVIEW

Outside the room where Malvolio has been confined, Maria impishly tells Feste to visit Malovolio disguised as Sir Topas, a priest. She gives Feste a gown and false beard to wear as she goes to bring Sir Toby. Feste agrees to go along with Maria's idea, but, alone, he is a little reluctant to take the prank so far. He puts on the gown and beard as Maria returns with Sir Toby, and he calls to Malvolio, identifying himself in a disguised voice as "Sir Topas the curate, who comes to visit Malvolio the lunatic." Malvolio insists that he is quite sane, but Feste keeps pulling his leg, playfully getting Malvolio into a foolish debate about Pythagoras and the doctrine of the reincarnation of the soul.

Sir Toby urges Feste to resume his natural voice. He thinks the prank on Malvolio has gone far enough—maybe a little too far, for it now risks making Olivia (who has high regard for her steward) angry. Now Feste sings to Malvolio in his own voice, but also speaks as Sir Topas, so that Malvolio thinks he is dealing with two separate men. Promising Feste a generous reward, Malvolio begs him for ink, paper, and light, so that he may prove his sanity to his lady.

ANALYSIS

In the final deception of the play, Feste impersonates a priest, under the name of Sir Topas, for the purpose of further befuddling Malvolio in his madman's cell. Malvolio thinks the clergyman will help him to get fair treatment, never suspecting that "Sir Topas" is merely a new addition to the conspiracy against him.

"LOVE SOUGHT IS GOOD, BUT GIVEN UNSOUGHT IS BETTER."

ACT IV, SCENE 3

OVERVIEW

Alone in Olivia's orchard, Sebastian is marveling at the pearl she has given him. He keeps repeating that what he is experiencing in the strange land of Illyria cannot be madness. But, he worries, where is his dear friend Antonio, who was supposed to meet him yesterday at the inn known as the Elephant? As Sebastian, who finds Olivia wholly admirable, tries to make some sense of the situation, Olivia arrives with a priest. She wants to marry Sebastian (whom she thinks is Cesario) in her chapel immediately. Sebastian happily agrees.

ANALYSIS

In this short scene, a major part of the plot is resolved: Olivia's passion for Cesario is satisfied by her marriage to Viola's twin brother Sebastian.

Shakespeare ends one of his most joyous plays with unexpected marital pairings, beginning with this one. Though these unions are more fantastic than realistic, we forgive their improbability because they are so romantic, entertaining, and dramatically apt. As Fabian has said earlier of the prank on Malvolio, "If this were played upon a stage now, I could condemn it as an improbable fiction." The Bard is well aware of how unlikely his whole story is, with its shipwreck, separated twins, mistaken identities, playful conspiracy, lucky love triangle, and coincidences. One of his characters comments on this so that the audience will not feel it is being asked to accept too much.

ACT V, SCENE 1

OVERVIEW

At Olivia's estate, Feste has Malvolio's letter to Olivia. Fabian wants to read it, but the fool refuses to let him, for it proves that Malvolio is perfectly sane and has been confined wrongly.

Orsino arrives with Viola, Curio, and some lords. After some of his typical banter, Feste leaves. Several officers bring Antonio in, under arrest, and Viola recognizes him as the man who saved her (in her Cesario guise) from Sir Andrew.

Meanwhile, Antonio is angry at Viola, as he mistakes her for her twin brother, Sebastian, who appears to have betrayed him.

Olivia enters with her attendants. She of course mistakes Viola for Cesario, and has accuses Cesario of betrayed her when "he" denies that he is her husband. Orsino blames Viola/Cesario for stealing the heart of Olivia, still the object of his love, and Olivia summons the priest to attest that she is betrothed to the supposed young man. The priest says that this is so.

Orsino becomes furious at Cesario, the "dissembling cub" whom he paid to help him court Olivia, but who betrayed him. Viola/Cesario tries to protest, but Sir Andrew arrives, calling for a surgeon for himself and Sir Toby. Both have been roughed up, it seems, by Cesario, but again Viola pleads innocent.

Now Sir Toby limps in, accompanied by Feste, complaining of his injury. As Sir Toby departs with Sir Andrew, Feste, and Fabian, Sebastian arrives and apologizes to Olivia for attacking her kinsman. Everyone is startled to see that he looks just like Cesario. Orsino and Antonio marvel at the resemblance first; then the twins themselves joyfully realize what has happened, and the whole company begins to comprehend. When Orsino sees that Cesario is actually a girl, his anger ceases and his fondness for his page turns into romantic love.

Feste enters with Fabian, and Olivia orders him to read Malvolio's letter aloud. He begins to do so, but in such a ridiculously unnatural voice that she orders Fabian to read it instead. The letter convinces Olivia that there is nothing wrong with her steward's mind, and she directs Fabian to release him from the cell. When Malvolio comes forth, he accuses Olivia of having done him "notorious wrong," then shows her the letter he thought she had written to him.

Olivia admits that it is a good imitation of her own penmanship, but says it is undoubtedly Maria's writing. She sees how the practical joke was born, and she promises the angry steward full redress of the wrongs he has suffered. Fabian owns up to his part in the plot, but he says Malvolio brought it on himself with his malicious speech; he also mentions that Sir Toby has married Maria in "recompense" for her role in the prank. Feste chimes in by reminding Malvolio of his earlier taunts and quoting passages from Maria's forgery. The humiliated steward goes out with a final threat: "I'll be revenged on the whole pack of you!" Olivia and Orsino take pity on him, and they send people to pacify him.

Feste is left alone, and he concludes the play with a song.

ANALYSIS

The play begins with music and unrequited love, and it ends with music and love fulfilled. Only one character—Malvolio—is excluded from the final festivities. In reality he excludes *himself* with his sour nature, which has made him an enemy of joy all along. Yet Shakespeare does not paint Malvolio as an evil man. True evil and malice can hardly exist in the enchanted world of *Twelfth Night*.

LIST OF CHARACTERS

Orsino—duke of Illyria

Valentine and Curio—gentlemen attending Orsino

Sir Toby Belch—uncle of Olivia

Sir Andrew Aguecheek—companion of Sir Toby, suitor of Olivia

Malvolio—Olivia's steward

Fabian—Olivia's servant

Feste—Olivia's jester

Sebastian—Viola's twin brother

Antonio—Sebastian's friend

Sea Captain, Priest, Officers, Musicians, Servants

Olivia—a rich countess

Viola—Sebastian's twin sister

Maria—Olivia's gentlewoman

ANALYSIS OF MAJOR CHARACTERS

VIOLA

Of all Shakespeare's heroines, Viola is one of the best loved. She is sweet, pure, loyal, quick-witted, and resourceful. Though she is cunning, she has no trace of cynicism, selfishness, or malice. Like all the Bard's finest creations, she is impossible to describe adequately. Her personality is so specific and lively that it must be known directly, not at second hand.

Though she disguises herself as a young man for innocent reasons, Viola comes to regard disguise as "a wickedness" that plays into the devil's hands. Yet only in her first scene does the audience see her dressed as a woman.

Incidentally, considering that in the English theater of that time, women's roles had to be played by males (usually boys), we can only marvel that Shakespeare wrote so many great female roles in both tragedy and comedy. Even today, these roles challenge some of the greatest actresses in the world.

ORSINO

At the beginning of the play Orsino is called a duke, but in the rest of the play, for some reason, he is referred to by the lesser title of count. He is a sentimental man whose professions of love for Olivia are too shallow to mean very much. When he learns that she has married Sebastian and that the supposed boy Cesario is really the girl Viola, he quickly transfers his affection to Viola. This being a comedy, we have to assume that they live happily ever after, no matter how unworthy of Viola he may seem to us.

OLIVIA

The first thing we learn of the countess Olivia is that she has made a rather silly decision to mourn her dead brother for seven years, during which time she will let no man see her. She instantly falls in love with Cesario and forgets this pledge. (In the plays of Shakespeare, such vows are made to be broken.) Olivia rules her household ably, relying on her capable steward Malvolio to enforce her orders and to pay for the anger they provoke.

MALVOLIO

The ill-tempered steward Malvolio, a born enemy of every kind of festivity, is the victim of a brilliant hoax, perfectly calculated to appeal to his secret vanity and to expose it for all to see. He even daydreams of marrying Olivia and becoming a count. All the other characters dislike him, and it is easy to see why they do. Yet in recent times actors, critics, and audiences

IMOGEN STUBBS, *LEFT*, AS VIOLA, AND HELENA BONHAM CARTER, *RIGHT*, AS OLIVIA, APPEARED IN THE 1996 FILM DIRECTED BY TREVOR NUNN.

have regarded Malvolio with more sympathy than Shakespeare may have intended. After all, he seems to be a man of honor and integrity, even if he is charmless. If he has no friends and inspires no affection, it is largely because he does his thankless duties so conscientiously. Fun-loving people are bound to find him disagreeable, especially a fun-loving character as irresponsible and parasitic as Sir Toby Belch.

For all that, Malvolio is a lonely figure, punished a little harshly for what are actually minor faults. Which of us, after all, could bear to have our daydreams revealed to the world as poor Malvolio's are?

FESTE

Olivia's jester's very name (which is used only once in the entire play) suggests festivity, so it is no wonder that he and Malvolio are spiritual enemies. Feste, we learn, has returned to Olivia's household after a long and unexplained absence.

Feste's humor is diverse: puns, playful insults, snatches of Latin, bogus quotations from fictitious ancient philosophers (whom he calls by such invented names as Quinapalus and Pigrogromitus), parodies, choplogic, paradoxes, and other forms of whimsy. Many of his jokes seem deliberately obscure, and scholars have never agreed on what some of them mean (if indeed they mean anything). We must beware of assuming that Shakespeare's language was always easy for Elizabethan audiences to understand. It was not. At times it must have been just as challenging for them as it is for us, and he meant it to be. The difficulty lies in the density, not just the period, of his language. Some of Shakespeare's finest and most admiring critics, such as Samuel Johnson, have complained that he is often needlessly obscure. (At times modern editors are unsure whether an obscure passage is what Shakespeare intended or is actually a misprint in the earliest edition!)

Feste quibbles constantly with the terms *fool, folly, wit, wisdom,* and *madness,* noting that words may be abused to prove almost anything. He is not Olivia's fool, he insists, but her "corrupter of words." And he deplores the modern abuse of words: "To see this age! A sentence is but a cheveril [soft leather] glove to a good wit. How quickly the wrong side may be turned outward!" He laments that "words are grown so false, I am loath to prove reason with them."

In his own humorous way, Feste is a truth seeker. He faces himself without illusions. When Orsino asks him how he is doing, he gives the puzzling reply, "Truly, sir, the better for my foes, and the worse for my friends." Surely, Orsino says, you mean just the contrary: "the better for thy friends." No, says Feste; "they praise me and make an ass of me. Now my foes tell me plainly that I am an ass; so that by my foes, sir, I profit in the knowledge of myself, and by my friends I am abused [deceived]; . . . why then, the worse for my friends, and the better for my foes."

SIR TOBY BELCH

The name of Olivia's uncle seems to imply both crudeness and corpulence. He is a useless parasite—a glutton and drunkard—who lives shamelessly off others, including his niece and the dull-witted Sir Andrew.

The earthy Sir Toby is often likened to Sir John Falstaff, but the resemblance is largely superficial. Falstaff has an immense superiority in wit, with a much deeper and warmer personality, capable of great pathos, in contrast to Sir Toby, who is merely a clever and shallow cynic. Nobody would call Sir Toby, vivid and funny as he is, one of Shakespeare's greatest creations; he has none of that seemingly infinite inventiveness of such characters as Falstaff, Hamlet, Cleopatra, and even the diabolical Iago. We can hardly imagine him in another setting or another play. He is best known for a single memorable taunt at Malvolio: "Dost thou think, because thou art virtuous, there shall be no more cakes and ale?"

SIR ANDREW AGUECHEEK

The well-to-do Sir Andrew, encouraged by Sir Toby, has come to woo Olivia, though he has no chance of winning her hand. He is egregiously stupid, as he himself is dimly aware: he observes, "Methinks sometimes I have no more wit than a Christian or an ordinary man has. But I am a great eater of beef, and I believe that does harm to my wit." He never suspects that Sir Toby is taking advantage of him for his money, and Sir Toby's jokes at his expense go right over his head.

Sir Andrew's vain desire for Olivia makes him one with two other failed suitors—Orsino and Malvolio—who also harbor dreams of possessing the rich countess until Sebastian suddenly appears and marries her. At the same time, Sebastian's flaring valor in the duel scene exposes Sir Andrew's comical cowardice.

We may well wonder what sort of woman would want to marry Sir Andrew. Yet he does have a single good quality: his obtusely cheerful nature.

A CLOSER LOOK

- THEMES

- MOTIFS

- SYMBOLS

- LANGUAGE

- INTERPRETING THE PLAY

A movie poster features ▶
the actors in the 1996 film
directed by Trevor Nunn.

Before Priscilla crossed the desert, *Wong Foo met Julie Newmar, and the Birdcage was unlocked, there was...*

Helena Bonham Carter
Richard E. Grant
Nigel Hawthorne
Ben Kingsley
Mel Smith
Imelda Staunton
Toby Stephens
Imogen Stubbs

Twelfth Night

Chapter Three

66929 66929

CHAPTER THREE

A Closer Look

THE DIFFERENCES BETWEEN THE SEXES

Twelfth Night's central character, Viola, the lovely girl disguised as a boy, combines both masculine and feminine virtues; so does her equally attractive twin brother, Sebastian. Shakespeare never suggests that the two sexes are interchangeable, however; he loves and delights in both as they are.

The play is also much concerned with wit and wisdom, on the one hand, and folly and madness on the other. It insists that fools and wise men are not always easy to tell apart.

THE ELUSIVENESS OF TRUTH

Viola is basically honest. She adopts a disguise only to protect herself in a strange country, not to take advantage of others. She tells the truth as much as possible, often indirectly, as when she tells Orsino of her fictitious sister who "never told her love," in effect describing her own secret love for Orsino. Feste the jester tells the truth indirectly too, in jokes, riddles, and parodies of scholarship, as when he playfully quotes an "old hermit of Prague, that never saw pen and ink, [who] very wittily said to a niece of King Gorboduc, 'That that is, is.'" The impish Feste does this sort of thing constantly. As the discerning Viola says of him, "This fellow is wise enough to play the fool."

DISGUISES AND RUSES

The play is full of deceits, disguises, and playful conspiracies. Viola deceives nearly everyone with her Cesario disguise. Maria, Sir Toby, and Fabian fool Malvolio with a forged letter; later Feste joins the fun by impersonating a priest. Sir Toby tricks Sir Andrew out of his money and then lures him into a duel with Cesario.

Antonio, a sea captain, mistakenly thinks Cesario/Viola is his friend Sebastian, whom he has befriended at great risk to himself and appears to have betrayed him. All these blunders are eventually resolved in concord, without tragedy.

Viola's identical twin brother, Sebastian, is mistaken for her; the results include a violent duel and a happy marriage to Olivia, who is enamored of Cesario, the boy she mistakes Viola for. Duke (or is he a count?) Orsino, meanwhile, upon learning that Cesario is actually a girl, falls in love with her and weds her.

MOTIFS

Several of the characters of *Twelfth Night* love word play. They jocularly cite Latin adages, supposed ancient authors, silly tautologies, and other fragments of humorous "learning." Sir Toby and Feste specialize in such word games, which are funny because they are usually so inappropriate to the occasion of their use; Feste—the self-styled "corrupter of words"—laments the abuse of language but then deliberately abuses it himself, just for fun. The priggish Malvolio disapproves of Feste's whimsical humor and, as we should expect, belittles and insults it. Sir Toby would enliven any celebration; but Malvolio, it seems safe to say, would be the death of the party.

SYMBOLS

As it so often does, water stands for disparate and even conflicting things: it can be both a nourisher and a destroyer of life. The sea produces the shipwreck that nearly drowns both Viola and Sebastian, casting both of them up on the coast of Illyria; yet Orsino, in the play's first speech, likens the sea to the spirit of love.

LANGUAGE

In this, one of Shakespeare's most charming works, his mastery of the English language is more casual than usual, with little of the spectacular eloquence of the great tragedies, but an easygoing assurance that makes the dialogue memorable. Even the names of the characters are suggestive: Malvolio is apt for a villain (though not everyone agrees that he is a villian), and Feste hints at festivity. Sir Toby Belch is suitably crude, as his name implies; he is hardly a refined or chivalrous specimen of knighthood. Viola is a delicate, flowerlike beauty—one of Shakespeare's most beloved heroines.

Consider a few of the play's most famous lines: Orsino's "If music be the food of love, play on," which opens the play; Sir Toby's "Dost thou think, because thou art virtuous, there shall be no more cakes and ale?"; Sir Andrew's sublimely imbecilic "I am a great eater of beef, and I believe that does harm to my wit"; Olivia's "Why, this is very midsummer madness"; the forged letter's "Some are born great, some achieve greatness, and some have greatness thrust upon them"; and many more. These are all common lines, still in use today, relying on none of the poet's awesome vocabulary for their effect. Shakespeare's simple good humor suffices. And all this does not even include the wondrous little songs, those plain and immortally haunting love ditties, written in monosyllables, which no other genius could have conceived.

INTERPRETING THE PLAY

Most scholars believe that *Twelfth Night* was written within a couple of years of *Julius Caesar*. If so, the fact illustrates the awesome range and versatility of Shakespeare's imagination, for it would be hard to name two plays so different as the romantic comedy set in the fantasy land of Illyria and the solemn historical tragedy of ancient Rome.

If the tragic plot seems driven by powerful, flawed characters, the plot of comedy seems determined by more benign forces: divine providence, supernatural intervention (think of Oberon, Titania, and Puck), magic or miracles (as in *The Tempest*), good luck, mere accident, or happy coincidence. The tragic hero typically brings his fate on himself. Even if he does not exactly deserve the disaster he helps to provoke, it has a certain fitness to his character, whether he is an evildoer like Macbeth or an essentially noble soul like Othello. In *Twelfth Night*, Viola is both a virtuous character and a very lucky one: she and her twin brother, Sebastian, both survive a shipwreck, and everything turns out happily for her. Even Sebastian's abrupt and unforeseeable marriage to Olivia is part of Viola's good fortune. In real life we would feel that such a marriage was rash and unwise, but in comedy we can be confident that everything will turn out all right. Comedy naturally moves toward marriage, joy, and festivity . . . "And they lived happily ever after."

In its early scenes, *Twelfth Night* touches briefly on the subject of death, but none of the characters we see are ever in real danger of dying. Illyria is a Never Never Land where fate is a kindly force and serious evil can hardly exist. We feel that tragedy is impossible there. If Malvolio can be called the play's villain, he is quite a harmless villain, and despite his name (which means "ill will"), he is not even malicious. In fact, he is the dupe and victim of the other characters, who make him their sport almost from the beginning. If his chief fault is, as Olivia says, "self-love," then his punishment is no worse than frustration and humiliation.

Far from illuminating readers, much of the modern criticism of *Twelfth Night* has been harder to understand than the play itself. In 1818 the great William Hazlitt offered the surprising opinion that the play is "perhaps too good-natured for comedy." A few years later, another famous commentator, Charles Lamb, wrote a noted defense of the character of Malvolio, denying that the Bard meant him to be a mere comic butt, but on the contrary gave him real pathos and dignity.

The play's title refers to the final night of the traditional Christmas season, the Feast of the Epiphany, and it is clear that the play's setting is Christian (even though some of the characters appeal to such pagan gods as Jove and Mercury): we hear of churches, a chantry, heaven and hell, fiends, and devils, and the characters include both a real and a fake priest.

And yet even this sweet and charming play has undertones of sadness and grief. Its first scene tells us of mourning; it has many references (both literal and figurative) to drowning; and its final lines remind us that "the rain it raineth every day."

Chronology

1564   William Shakespeare is born on April 23 in Stratford-upon-Avon, England

1578–1582   Span of Shakespeare's "Lost Years," covering the time between leaving school and marrying Anne Hathaway of Stratford

1582   At age eighteen Shakespeare marries Anne Hathaway, age twenty-six, on November 28

1583   Susanna Shakespeare, William and Anne's first child, is born in May, six months after the wedding

1584   Birth of twins Hamnet and Judith Shakespeare

1585–1592   Shakespeare leaves his family in Stratford to become an actor and playwright in a London theater company

1587   Public beheading of Mary Queen of Scots

1593–1594   The Bubonic (Black) Plague closes theaters in London

1594–1596   As a leading playwright, Shakespeare creates some of his most popular work, including *A Midsummer Night's Dream* and *Romeo and Juliet*

1596   Hamnet Shakespeare dies in August at age eleven, possibly of plague

1596–1597	*The Merchant of Venice* and *Henry IV, Part One* most likely are written
1599	The Globe Theater opens
1600	*Julius Caesar* is first performed at the Globe
1600–1601	*Hamlet* is believed to have been written
1601–1602	*Twelfth Night* is probably composed
1603	Queen Elizabeth dies; Scottish king James VI succeeds her and becomes England's James I
1604	Shakespeare pens *Othello*
1605	*Macbeth* is composed
1608–1610	London's theaters are forced to close when the plague returns and kills an estimated 33,000 people
1611	*The Tempest* is written
1613	The Globe Theater is destroyed by fire
1614	Reopening of the Globe
1616	Shakespeare dies on April 23
1623	Anne Hathaway, Shakespeare's widow, dies; a collection of Shakespeare's plays, known as the First Folio, is published

Source Notes

p. 10, par. 5, Asquith, Clare. *Shadowplay: The Hidden Beliefs and Coded Politics of William Shakespeare.* (New York: PublicAffairs/Perseus Books Group, 2006).

p. 31, par. 2, Jonson, Ben. "To the Memory of My Beloved, The Author, Mr. William Shakespeare, And What He Hath Left Us." In *Poetry X*, 4 Sep 2004, http://poetry.poetryx.com/poems/5271/

p. 39, par. 2, Booth, Stephen. *Precious Nonsense: The Gettysburg Address, Jonson's Epitaphs on His Children, and Twelfth Night.* (Berkeley: University of California Press, 1998).

p. 72, par. 5, Booth, *Precious Nonsense.* The three chapters on *Twelfth Night* are titled *Twelfth Night* 1.1: The Audience as Malvolio; Getting into the Spirit of *Twelfth Night:* The Audience as Malvolio Again; and, The Last Few Minutes of *Twelfth Night.*

p. 74, par. 1, Samuel Johnson was an eighteenth-century English poet, critic, biographer, and lexicographer. See *A Dictionary of the English Language: An Anthology* (New York: Penguin Classics, 2007) for examples of language usage in Shakespeare's work.

p. 75, par. 2, See John Dover Wilson's *The Fortunes of Falstaff.* (Cambridge: Cambridge University Press, 1979) for a stimulating study of Shakespeare's greatest comic character.

p. 82, par. 2, See William Hazlitt's *Characters in Shakespeare's Plays,* (Charleston, SC: BiblioBazaar, 2006) and *Charles Lamb on Shakespeare* (Buckinghamshire, UK: Colin Smythe, 1978).

A Shakespeare Glossary

The student should not try to memorize these, but only refer to them as needed. We can never stress enough that the best way to learn Shakespeare's language is simply to *hear* it—to hear it spoken well by good actors. After all, small children master every language on earth through their ears, without studying dictionaries, and we should master Shakespeare, as much as possible, the same way.

addition — a name or title (knight, duke, duchess, king, etc.)
admire — to marvel
affect — to like or love; to be attracted to
an — if ("An I tell you that, I'll be hanged.")
approve — to prove or confirm
attend — to pay attention
belike — probably
beseech — to beg or request
betimes — soon; early
bondman — a slave
bootless — futile; useless; in vain
broil — a battle
charge — expense, responsibility; to command or accuse
clepe, clept — to name; named
common — of the common people; below the nobility
conceit — imagination
condition — social rank; quality
countenance — face; appearance; favor
cousin — a relative
cry you mercy — beg your pardon
curious — careful; attentive to detail
dear — expensive
discourse — to converse; conversation
discover — to reveal or uncover
dispatch — to speed or hurry; to send; to kill
doubt — to suspect

entreat — to beg or appeal

envy — to hate or resent; hatred; resentment

ere — before

ever, e'er — always

eyne — eyes

fain — gladly

fare — to eat; to prosper

favor — face, privilege

fellow — a peer or equal

filial — of a child toward its parent

fine — an end; in fine = in sum

fond — foolish

fool — a darling

genius — a good or evil spirit

gentle — well-bred; not common

gentleman — one whose labor was done by servants (Note: to call someone a *gentleman* was not a mere compliment on his manners; it meant that he was above the common people.)

gentles — people of quality

get — to beget (a child)

go to — "go on"; "come off it"

go we — let us go

haply — perhaps

happily — by chance; fortunately

hard by — nearby

heavy — sad or serious

husbandry — thrift; economy

instant — immediate

kind — one's nature; species

knave — a villain; a poor man

lady — a woman of high social rank (Note: *lady* was not a synonym for *woman* or *polite woman*; it was not a compliment, but, like *gentleman,* simply a word referring to one's actual legal status in society.)

leave — permission; "take my leave" = depart (with permission)

lief, lieve — "I had as lief" = I would just as soon; I would rather

like — to please; "it likes me not" = it is disagreeable to me

livery — the uniform of a nobleman's servants; emblem
mark — notice; pay attention
morrow — morning
needs — necessarily
nice — too fussy or fastidious
owe — to own
passing — very
peculiar — individual; exclusive
privy — private; secret
proper — handsome; one's very own ("his proper son")
protest — to insist or declare
quite — completely
require — request
several — different; various
severally — separately
sirrah — a term used to address social inferiors
sooth — truth
state — condition; social rank
still — always; persistently
success — result(s)
surfeit — fullness
touching — concerning; about; as for
translate — to transform
unfold — to disclose
villain — a low or evil person; originally, a peasant
voice — a vote; consent; approval
vouchsafe — to confide or grant
vulgar — common
want — to lack
weeds — clothing
what ho — "hello, there!"
wherefore — why
wit — intelligence; sanity
withal — moreover; nevertheless
without — outside
would — wish

Suggested Essay Topics

1. Discuss the elements of sadness and melancholy in *Twelfth Night*.

2. Is Malvolio the villain of *Twelfth Night*? Why or why not?

3. Compare and contrast Sir Toby Belch and Sir John Falstaff.

4. How does Feste view the other characters of *Twelfth Night*?

5. *Twelfth Night* ends with Orsino hoping to mollify Malvolio. Is this likely to happen? Why or why not?

Testing Your Memory

1. How long does Olivia intend to mourn her dead brother? a) a year; b) a month; c) forever; d) seven years.

2. Viola's original plan is to disguise herself as a) a boy; b) a knight; c) a sailor; d) a eunuch.

3. Sir Toby is Olivia's a) steward; b) wooer; c) uncle; d) jester.

4. Sir Andrew has come to Olivia's household in the hope of a) getting rich; b) marrying her; c) reveling; d) dancing.

5. Sir Andrew is supposedly skilled in a) speaking foreign languages; b) fencing; c) charming the opposite sex; d) playing chess.

6. To what does Sir Andrew attribute his own weak wit? a) beef; b) drinking; c) idleness; d) bad company.

7. How long does it take Viola to win Orsino's full confidence? a) an hour; b) a week; c) three days; d) three months.

8. Feste has just returned from a) a journey to Italy; b) an unexplained absence; c) exile; d) England.

9. Quinapalus is a) a kinsman of Orsino; b) a sea captain; c) an ancient Roman warrior; d) an imaginary philosopher.

10. What is Malvolio's attitude toward Feste? a) affection; b) resentment; c) contempt; d) jealousy.

11. Sebastian and Viola are a) lovers; b) enemies; c) twins; d) old friends.

12. When we first meet Sebastian, his chief interest is a) Viola's fate; b) Olivia's dowry; c) Sir Andrew's wealth; d) Orsino's dukedom.

13. Maria scornfully likens Malvolio to a) a pickpocket; b) a puritan; c) a police agent; d) a politician.

14. Malvolio is deceived by a) a lie; b) the twins; c) a messenger from Orsino; d) a forged letter.

15. Who does Malvolio think wrote the letter to him? a) Maria; b) Viola; c) Rosalind; d) Olivia.

16. Name the source of these famous words: "Some are born great, some achieve greatness, and some have greatness thrust upon 'em." a) Viola; b) Sir Toby; c) Malvolio; d) Maria.

17. Who risks his life to help Sebastian? a) Antonio; b) Feste; c) Orsino; d) Cesario.

18. Sir Topas is a) a drinking companion of Sir Toby and Sir Andrew; b) Feste in the disguise of a priest; c) Orsino's bodyguard; d) a steward.

19. Who finally marries Olivia? a) Sebastian; b) Cesario; c) Orsino; d) Sir Andrew.

20. Whom does Maria finally marry? a) Malvolio; b) Sir Toby; c) Feste; d) Fabian.

Answer Key

1. d); 2. d); 3. c); 4. b); 5. a); 6. a); 7. c); 8. b); 9. d); 10. c); 11. c); 12. a); 13. b); 14. d); 15. d); 16.d); 17. a); 18. b); 19. a); 20. b)

Further Information

BOOKS

Ackroyd, Peter. *Shakespeare: The Biography*. New York: Nan A. Talese, 2005.

Dunton-Downer, Leslie, and Alan Riding. *The Essential Shakespeare Handbook*. New York, Dorling-Kindersley, 2004.

Graphic Shakespeare series. *Twelfth Night*. Minneapolis: Magic Wagon Books, 2008.

The Oxford Shakespeare *Twelfth Night*. New York: Oxford University Press, 2008.

WEBSITES

Absolute Shakespeare is a resource for the Bard's plays, sonnets, and poems and includes summaries, quotes, films, trivia, and more. http://absoluteshakespeare.com

Play Shakespeare: The Ultimate Free Shakespeare Resource features all the play texts with an online glossary, reviews, a discussion forum, and links to festivals worldwide. http://www.playshakespeare.com

The Shakespeare Resource Center provides a vast collection of links to assist in online research; click on Ask the Bard for "burning questions."

FILMS

Twelfth Night, directed by Trevor Nunn; with Helena Bonham Carter, Richard E. Grant, Imogen Stubbs, et al., 1996.

AUDIO CD

Twelfth Night, Arkangel Shakespeare/BBC Audio Books, 2005.

RECORDING

Twelfth Night, Caedmon; with Paul Scofield as Malvolio.

Bibliography

General Commentary

Bate, Jonathan, and Eric Rasmussen, eds. *William Shakespeare Complete Works (Modern Library)*. New York: Random House, 2007.

Bloom, Harold. *Shakespeare: The Invention of the Human*. New York: Riverhead Books,1998.

Garber, Marjorie. *Shakespeare After All*. New York: Pantheon, 2004.

Goddard, Harold C. *The Meaning of Shakespeare*. Chicago: University of Chicago Press, 1951.

Traversi, D. L. *An Approach to Shakespeare*. Palo Alto, CA: Stanford University Press, 1957.

Van Doren, Mark. *Shakespeare*. Garden City, NY: Doubleday, 1939.

Biography

Burgess, Anthony. *Shakespeare*. New York: Alfred A. Knopf, 1970.

Chute, Marchette. *Shakespeare of London*. New York: Dutton, 1949.

Greenblatt, Stephen. *Will in the World: How Shakespeare Became Shakespeare*. New York: W. W. Norton & Company, 2004.

Honan, Park. *Shakespeare: A Life*. New York: Oxford University Press, 1998.

Schoenbaum, Samuel. *William Shakespeare: A Documentary Life*. New York: Oxford University Press, 1975.

———. *William Shakespeare: Records and Images*. New York: Oxford University Press, 1981.

Index

Page numbers in **boldface** are illustrations.

About the Author

Joseph Sobran is the author of several books, including *Alias Shakespeare* (1997). He lives in northern Virginia.